History of Europe

1500-1848

About the Author

Henry W. Littlefield is President of the University of Bridgeport, Connecticut. He received the degrees of B.S. and M.A. at New York University and the degree of Ph.D. at Yale University. He has been visiting professor in the field of social sciences at the University of Maryland and has contributed to the development of programs of higher education in Connecticut, serving on the staff of New Haven College and the Connecticut State Department of Education. Since 1962 he has served as Vice President of the Dana Foundation. He has held many positions of leadership in professional associations and organizations and has served as president of the American Association of Junior Colleges and of the Connecticut Council of Higher Education. He has also been a director of various educational agencies, such as the National Commission on Accrediting, the Learning Resources Institute, and the Museum of Arts, Sciences and Industry. Dr. Littlefield is the author of another College Outline, *History of Europe since 1815*.

COLLEGE OUTLINE SERIES

History of Europe
1500-1848

HENRY W. LITTLEFIELD

Fifth Edition

BARNES & NOBLE Inc. • NEW YORK

PUBLISHERS • BOOKSELLERS • SINCE 1873

Preface

The fifth edition of this outline of modern European history has been thoroughly revised and substantially enlarged. It deliberately overlaps the succeeding volume (Since 1815) so as to include the various beginning dates of the major textbooks in current use. The features of previous editions that have commended the book to students and teachers throughout the country have been preserved, and a large amount of new material has been added.

Throughout the book stress has been laid on the social and economic undercurrents that relate previous centuries so closely to the twentieth; with this end in view the chapter on the Industrial Revolution has been entirely rewritten.

In previous editions considerable care was taken to provide: (a) a convenient manual for daily reference and review, with concisely digested and clearly organized factual material, functional maps, selected bibliographies, a chronological summary, and other essential reference aids; (b) a practical handbook for the multiple-text courses now given in so many universities; (c) an organized compendium of political and social history to accompany histories of Western civilization; and (d) a comprehensive digest for literature courses or any study needing a concise treatment of historical background.

The Outline is adaptable to any of the leading college texts in modern European history. But it is not intended as a short-cut to, or a substitute for, the extensive reading of text and collateral material through which alone history can be learned. The Outline is a tool by which the student can review and coördinate the essential facts, and can construct in his mind a framework into which he can fit the fruits of further study.

—H. W. L.

Acknowledgments

In the preparation and revision of the *New Outline History of Europe, 1500-1848,* the author has been assisted by the helpful criticisms of many college instructors and students who have volunteered valuable suggestions for improving previous editions. Obligations to all of these cannot, for lack of space, be specifically acknowledged here; but for generous aid especial gratitude must be expressed to Mr. John Collins. The author is also indebted to Professor Bailey W. Diffie of the College of the City of New York for his painstaking reading and criticism of the galley proofs; to Miss Ella Wood of the English Department in Hamden, Connecticut, for her minute checking of the manuscript for consistency in punctuation and rhetoric; and to Miss Mildred Woods, for her exacting work in typing the manuscript. A special word of appreciation is due to Mr. Edward Fitzgerald, formerly of the Art Department of Barnes & Noble, Inc., who has contributed materially to the value of this volume by his extensive research and skillful execution of the series of excellent functional maps.

—H. W. L.

Table of Contents

Numbers in Parentheses Refer to Pages

Table of Contents (Cont'd.)

Table of Contents (Cont'd.)

Maps

TABULATED BIBLIOGRAPHY
of STANDARD TEXTBOOKS

The following list gives author, title, date, and publisher of the standard textbooks referred to in the table on the two succeeding pages.

Brace, Richard M., *The Making of the Modern World.* 2nd ed. enlarged. New York: Holt, Rinehart and Winston, 1961.

Bruun, G., and H. S. Commager, *Europe and America Since 1492.* Boston: Houghton Mifflin, 1954.

Burns, E. M., *Western Civilizations.* 6th ed. New York: Norton, 1963.

Ergang, R., *Europe from the Renaissance to Waterloo.* Boston: D. C. Heath, 1954.

Ferguson, Wallace K., and Geoffrey Bruun, *A Survey of European Civilization.* 3rd ed. 1962 impression. Boston: Houghton Mifflin, 1962.

Hayes, Carlton J. H., Marshall W. Baldwin, and Charles W. Cole, *History of Western Civilization Since 1500.* New York: Macmillan, 1962.

Palmer, R. R., and Joel Colton, *A History of the Modern World.* 2nd ed. New York: Knopf, 1956.

Schevill, Ferdinand, *A History of Europe from the Reformation to the Present Day.* Rev. ed. New York: Harcourt, Brace, 1951.

Stearns, Raymond Phineas, *Pageant of Europe.* Rev. ed. New York: Harcourt, Brace and World, 1961.

Wallbank, T. W., and A. M. Taylor, *Civilization Past and Present.* Vol. II. 4th ed. Chicago: Scott, Foresman, 1960.

QUICK REFERENCE TABLE TO STANDARD TEXTBOOKS

All numbers refer to pages

CHAPTER IN THIS OUTLINE	TOPIC	BRACE	BRUUN & COMMAGER	BURNS	ERGANG	FERGUSON & BRUUN	HAYES, BALDWIN & COLE	PALMER & COLTON	SCHEVILL	STEARNS	WALLBANK & TAYLOR
I	Europe on the Eve of Modern Times	1-61	35-41	311-345	1-39	xxxii-xxxviii 354-364	1-16	60-68 89-94	65-90	1-6	
II	Europe Socially and Economically in 1500	62-101 175-202	42-58	335-345 503-513	96-133	341-344 364-370	73-74	94-104	13-32 50-61	71-89	
III	Europe Politically in the 16th Century	156-163 175-203	67-97 152-160	514-545	146-175 261-274 317-392	389-398 409-419	49-60	104-113	139-150 178-190 196-210	91-98 158-188	
IV	Europe Religiously in the 16th Century	131-155 163-171 346-352	59-66	438-483	176-221 241-242	373-387 400-408	17-48	68-88	91-138 151-177	90-158	
V	Europe Culturally in the 16th Century	102-130 218-221 259-266 320-324	18-26	415-437 546-583	40-95 253-260 358-364 408-410	332-338 346-349 467-469 474-480	46-48	49-60	32-50 96-98 234-248	6-71	
VI	Rise of Parliament in England	222-238 309-332	138-151	514-595 711-720	380-408 411-498 546-550	419-422 431-441 513-524	167-180	142-155	261-288 340-348	215-239	20-24
VII	Development of Absolutism in France	198-208	76-78	720-728	322-336 342-350	423-430 442-449	63-80	113-131	207-233 289-291	186-188 240-247	7-14
VIII	Age of Louis XIV, 1661-1715	209-221	125-137	525-530	458-486	497-512	81-97	155-172	291-303	247-270	14-20

See page xi for list of complete titles.

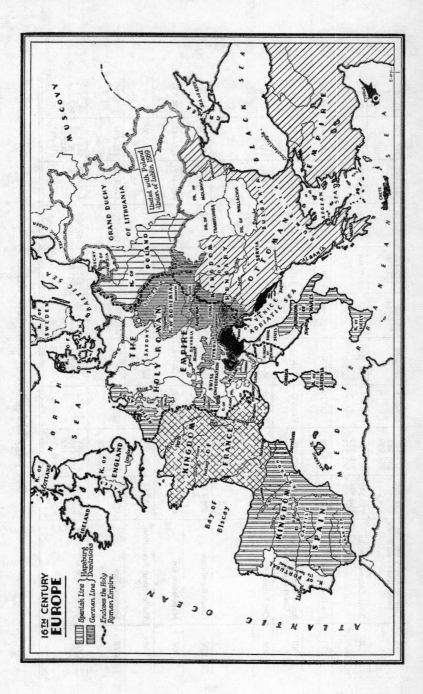

Significant Dates

Union of Calmar 1397

Accession of Louis XI . . 1461

Hapsburgs Dominate Netherlands 1477

Accession of Henry VII . . 1485

Charles VIII Invades Italy 1494

CHAPTER I.

EUROPE ON THE EVE OF MODERN TIMES

SIGNIFICANCE OF THE DATE 1500

The past of the human race is a continuous story, and our division of history into periods for convenience of study is in some respects a dangerous practice. It tends to fix in our minds an illusory notion of disconnectedness in human affairs and to make us exaggerate the importance of particular events. Although it was long the custom of historical writers to divide ancient and medieval history at the conventional date 476 A.D.—the date of the "fall" of the Roman Empire in the West — scholars, who made this division, knew that the comparatively insignificant event commemorated had practically nothing to do with the movement that over a course of centuries gradually transformed European civilization from Graeco-Roman to medieval, but the date became sanctified by repeated use and created a kind of historical myth that up to 476 A.D. we have "ancient history" while after 476 we have "medieval history." Similar myths have crystallized about two dates often used as the dividing line between medieval and modern times. The dates often quoted are 1453, when Constantinople was captured by the Ottoman Turks, and 1492, when Columbus discovered the New World. Both of these events

1

were important, but the transition from medieval to modern times was an evolutional historical process extending over centuries, and was not dependent upon any single event or any single economic, social, or cultural force. During the century extending roughly from 1450 to 1550 a comparatively rapid development occurred along many lines, and there was a conspicuous transformation in institutions and attitudes; together these evidences of change make up what we may call the Medieval-Modern Revolution. But this revolution was a drawn-out process, and its different elements changed at uneven rates and reacted upon each other in a most complex manner. Since, therefore, any date selected for the beginning of the modern period can be only suggestive, it is better to use a date such as 1500, the beginning of a new century, rather than the date of a particular event.

MAIN ELEMENTS OF THE MEDIEVAL-MODERN REVOLUTION

Intellectual and Cultural. The close of the Middle Ages is marked by those great changes in the intellectual atmosphere of Europe that have long been known by the general name "Renaissance." The Renaissance was characterized by (1) a notable revival of interest in and appreciation of the classics of Latin and Greek literature, (2) the humanist movement, a turning away from the medieval preoccupation with theology and asceticism toward a lively enjoyment of natural beauty and the earthly activities of man, (3) the rise of a spirit of inquiry, skepticism, and criticism, and (4) a broadening of intellectual interests, greatly stimulated by the invention of printing and the discovery of the New World.

Economic. Continually interacting with the intellectual movement was the rapidly expanding commercial life of Europe that led to the great explorations of the late fifteenth and early sixteenth centuries and began the spread of European civilization over the whole world. This commercial revolution brought a change from the self-sufficient, agricultural, practically static economy of the Middle Ages to the interdependent, commercial-agricultural, developing economy of the next three centuries and laid the groundwork for the Industrial Revolution of the nineteenth century.

Political. The rise of strong centralized monarchial states, based on national unity, and the breakdown of the feudalism of the Middle Ages is one of the most important developments of the modern period. The first nations to attain unity under such national governments were Portugal, Spain (Castile and Aragon), England, France, and the Netherlands. It is no mere coincidence that these nations are also the great empire-building nations of modern times. It is not even far-fetched to say that it was Germany's and Italy's failure to attain national unity in the sixteenth century that made them the great "have-not" nations of the twentieth.

Religious. The fourth great element in the transition movement from medieval to modern times was the break-up of the religious unity of Europe under the Roman Catholic Church. Previously, the Church had occupied a preëminent position, not only in religious matters, but also in certain aspects of the political, cultural, and economic spheres. With its far-reaching organization for spiritual control (see Chapter IV), the Church delved into temporal matters. As a result of a popular support built upon its moral influence, its vast holdings in land, and its other evidences of material wealth, political leaders had long recognized the superior authority of the Church. The real despotism of the medieval era was found in the Church. Therefore changes in the religious solidarity affected practically all areas of man's endeavors.

EUROPEAN NATIONAL MONARCHIES IN 1500

Portugal. Portugal reached its present boundaries in 1263 and by 1500 was an important European state. As a result of a bourgeois revolution in 1383-1385, a candidate supported by the merchants was placed upon the throne of Portugal, and political freedom from Spain was an accomplished fact. The defeat of the nobles' candidate in the bourgeois revolution made it possible for the king to dominate the situation, and the Cortes ceased to meet regularly after 1521. Prince Henry the Navigator (1394-1460) augmented Portugal's prestige by the advances he made in the science of navigation and by successful exploration abroad.

Spain (Castile and Aragon). The marriage of Ferdinand of Aragon and Isabella of Castile established a formal consolidation of Spain. The fall of Granada in 1492 ended the Mohammedan power. With the support of the middle class, Ferdinand and Isabella constantly increased their power and decreased that of the Cortes, the Spanish representative bodies. But Spain remained a much less united and homogenous state than France or England. Conflicting racial, religious, and linguistic groups, strong feelings of local pride, and a weaker commercial class combined to make the appearance of unity under an ambitious sovereign like Ferdinand more impressive than the reality. It was their desire to promote national unity as well as their religious bigotry that led Ferdinand and Isabella to institute the formidable Spanish Inquisition (1480), to expel the Jews (1492), and to persecute the Moors.

England. In England a strong national monarchy was established under the shrewd and energetic King, Henry VII (1485-1509), the first of the Tudor line, who secured the throne at the end of a long period of civil war (Wars of the Roses, 1455-1485). Among the factors working to promote a centralized government may be noted (1) the exhaustion and impoverishment of the rival factions of the nobility in the Wars of the Roses, (2) the rising influence of the bourgeoisie, or mercantile class living chiefly in the towns, who were determined on peace and order and were therefore willing to support a strong man who could suppress the turbulent barons, (3) the growth of national consciousness, which for two centuries had been corroding the old feudalism and had been notably stimulated by the series of national wars with France (Hundred Years' War, 1337-1453), and (4) the increase of wealth and trade with its consequences of greater travel and intermingling of the population. Henry VII was admirably fitted by temperament and ability to take advantage of this favorable atmosphere. He ruthlessly put down disorder, abstained from foreign war, and adopted a policy of fostering commerce through loans to merchants, by forbidding the exportation of bullion, and by fixing wages and prices. This served to strengthen his hand with the rising middle class. By a system of fines, confiscations, and forced loans he raised money without regular taxes and thus managed to make the crown financially independent of Parliament. By his economical management he amassed a large surplus in his treasury and thus passed on to his successor, Henry VIII, the means of continuing the despotic regime.

France. The work of unification and strengthening of the central government, performed in England by Henry VII, was accomplished in France largely by the cruel and unscrupulous but able King Louis XI (1461-1483). The same conditions that have been outlined as tending to the rise of a strong monarchy for England were also at work in France. The Estates-General, analogous to the English Parliament, was much less powerful in France, as the former lacked the long English tradition of resistance to the crown that had begun in England with the extortion of the Magna Carta from King John in 1215. Louis XI ignored the Estates-General in the crucial matter of levying taxes and ruled as an absolute tyrant. Like Henry VII he depended for support on the rising bourgeoisie, or commercial class, and he did much to stimulate trade by opening market places and encouraging the growth of the recently annexed Mediterranean port, Marseilles. Louis' son and successor, Charles VIII, by his grandiose project for the conquest of Italy and the establishment of France as the successor to the old Roman Empire, began a new era in French history marked by a policy of aggressive national expansion. In 1494 Charles invaded Italy, and for nearly half a century successive French kings continued to pursue Charles' policy. In many respects this Italian expedition of Charles marks the opening of the age of national power politics in European history, and thus might be as legitimately taken as the dividing point between Medieval and Modern history as the dates 1453 or 1492.

HOLY ROMAN EMPIRE

Unlike the new national states, the Holy Roman Empire had scarcely more than a theoretical unity. It claimed, indeed, a general suzerainty over all the Christian princes of Europe, but these claims were not recognized. For practical purposes the Holy Roman Empire was a loose association of German princes under the nominal leadership of an elected emperor. Three hundred feudal states, which are spoken of collectively as the

"Germanies," made up the Holy Roman Empire in 1500. At its head was the emperor elected by the seven electors of Brandenburg, Saxony, Trier, Mainz, Cologne, Rhine, and Bohemia. The Diet was composed of three houses made up of (1) seven electors (three of whom were archbishops), (2) the lesser princes and representatives of the clergy, and (3) free city representatives. The lack of harmony between the emperor, the electors, and the diet prevented national unity. As early as 1273 the Hapsburgs (Habsburgs) under Rudolph became emperors of the Holy Roman Empire which position they held almost continuously until its extinction under Napoleon (1806). Attempts at consolidation such as one made at the Diet of Worms (1495) were for the most part unsuccessful. As a matter of fact, the political unification of Germany was not accomplished for nearly 400 years.

CITY STATES IN ITALY AND THE NETHERLANDS

Italy. There was no political unity in Italy and little pretense of allegiance to the Holy Roman Empire because of (1) the Pope's opposition to national unity, (2) local independence due to commercial success, and (3) local jealousies. Increased commerce caused important trading centers to spring up in Northern Italy. These towns took the political form of the city states of Ancient Greece. The most important were Milan, Genoa, Venice, and Florence. At the opening of the sixteenth century Italy was the prey of rival invaders — French, German, Spanish — while the struggle for aggrandizement of the various petty despots produced a veritable anarchy. But in spite of these unsettled conditions, Italy was the intellectual and artistic center of Europe.

Netherlands. As in Italy, the city state was the political unit in the Netherlands, that is, Holland, Belgium, and the present Northern France. Among the leaders in commerce and industry were Antwerp, Brussels, Ghent, Liege, Rotterdam, and Utrecht. In spite of the political change which finally placed the Hapsburgs in the commanding position over the Netherlands in 1477, the city states retained considerable freedom and prospered more than ever.

OTHER EUROPEAN COUNTRIES

Scandinavian Countries. Denmark, Norway, and Sweden were loosely joined together by the Union of Calmar (1397), but Sweden became independent in 1523, whereas Norway and Denmark continued united until 1814.

Russia. The Russians were one of that group of Slavic peoples which included the Poles, Lithuanians, Czechs, and Balkans. Unlike that of other European States, the civilization of the Russians was predominately Eastern. Even Russia's Christianity was derived from Constantinople. At the beginning of the sixteenth century there was little contact between western Europe and the Slavs in the east. But the Russians under their able Grand Duke, Ivan III the Great, (1462-1505) were slowly building up a united nation. In 1478 Ivan conquered and annexed the republic of Novgorod and thus added the whole of northern Russia from Lapland to the Urals to the the Muscovite domain. In 1480 he refused further tribute payment to the Mongol or Tartar Grand Khan. By his marriage in 1472 with Sophia, a niece of the last Byzantine emperor, he laid the foundation of a claim to be the legitimate successor of the Roman Empire in the East.

Poland. Poland was a weak monarchy in 1500 because of (1) a heterogeneous population, (2) a lack of natural boundaries, (3) an unhampered feudalism, and (4) an ineffectual representative system.

Hungary. As in Poland, the presence in Hungary of a strong noble class, securely embedded in feudalism, prevented concentration of power in the hands of the king. The presence of strong neighbors, the Germans of Austria and the Holy Roman Empire, the Vlachs, Greeks, Slavs, and finally the Ottoman Turks, occupied the kings with foreign struggles and prevented internal consolidation. In the latter half of the fifteenth century, under the vigorous leadership of John Hunyadi (1387-1456) and his son Matthias Corvinus (1440-1490), Hungary seemed for a time to be on the road to national unity on the western pattern, but the movement proved to be only temporary. A period of decline set in upon Matthias' death, and in 1526 Hungarian independence was practically ended when an invasion of the Ottoman Turks destroyed the Hungarian army at the battle of Mohács.

Ottoman Empire. The Ottoman Turks, who were Asiatic Mohammedans, controlled the former Eastern Roman Empire, capturing Constantinople in 1453. These Turks conquered lands and although in some instances they ruled through Christian Patriarchs of the Church, yet their pressure up the Danube Valley and the expansion of their power over the eastern Mediterranean presented a constant threat to Christian Europe. However, the Christians had a greater degree of autonomy than Moslems received in Christian lands. The Patriarchs collected the taxes, judged the people, made the local laws and in general appeared to their parishioners as the real rulers. The Ottoman Turks established mosques and schools in the newly conquered territories.

CHAPTER II.

EUROPE SOCIALLY
AND ECONOMICALLY IN 1500

SOCIAL CLASSES

Nobility. In spite of the rapid growth during the fourteenth and fifteenth centuries of the bourgeoisie or town-dwelling class composed of shopkeepers, merchants, and professional persons, the bulk of the European population at the opening of the sixteenth century still depended directly on agriculture for their means of living. At the top of the social system stood the lay nobles and princes of the Church, who owned the land and were entitled to receive rents and dues from the peasantry. Their superior position, which had been obtained in return for protecting the king, the peasants, and the country against foes, was retained; although they no longer fulfilled these obligations. The ascendency of the king was gradually turning the nobility into a leisure class.

Peasantry. The peasantry was composed of the great mass of the people who earned their bread by working with their hands. By the sixteenth century the peasantry had broken up into many groups.

9

SERFS. The largest number of peasants in eastern and central Europe were still serfs — men bound to the soil. Some of the major obligations of the serf to his master were (a) part-time labor for his lord, (b) payment of certain feudal dues, (c) payment in kind for the use of his lord's gristmills and wine presses, and (d) a kind of inheritance tax. In western Europe this rigorous serfdom had greatly declined by the opening of the sixteenth century. Most of the peasant class in England, France, and the low countries had become free-tenants, hired laborers or métayers.

FREE-TENANTS. Some of the peasants were not required to give part-time labor to the lord, were free to leave the estates, to marry, and to sell their personal property without the consent of the lord. Such peasants were called free-tenants and they considered their dues as rent for their land.

HIRED LABORERS. One group found it necessary to become hired laborers, forfeiting their strips of land and working in the lord's fields for a fixed wage.

MÉTAYERS. Some of the peasants known as métayers worked farms which were owned and stocked by the nobles and in return paid a fixed percentage of their crops to the owners.

Condition of the Peasantry. Even the free peasants still had to fulfill certain feudal obligations, such as the payment of fees for use of the lord's mill, and their crops were at the mercy of the lord's hunting parties. The three-field system of agriculture persisted. Primitive implements and a lack of knowledge in the care of land and the breeding of cattle resulted in small crops and inferior animals. The peasants lived in their own world of disease, plagues, and famines; the lords, in theirs of ease, luxury, and plenty; and only in the church of the manor did they approach common ground. It is difficult for the modern student to appreciate the rigidity of the class stratification that prevailed. Practically all the peasants were illiterate, and they had no means and little hope of rising out of the class into which they were born. They accepted without complaint a life of hard labor and grinding poverty that would seem to a modern man impossible to endure. From time to time in the late middle ages there were formidable peasant insurrections such as the rising of the English lower classes under Wat Tyler and John Ball (1381), the rebellion of the French peasants known as the Jacquerie (1358), and greatest of all, the German Peasants' Revolt (1525), but these uprisings were provoked by special combinations of local circumstances and should not be taken as representing any real revolutionary spirit pervading the European peasant class as a whole. For the most part, the rural communities were strongholds of conservatism. Far less than the commercial towns were they affected by the "contact of cultures" — the comparing and intermingling of customs and social institutions — that followed the increase of travel and trade in the fourteenth and fifteenth centuries.

Bourgeoisie. Although they comprised only a small minority of the population, their growing power and vitality at the opening of the sixteenth century gives a special importance to the bourgeoisie, or town dwellers. In many respects the whole of modern history may be looked upon as the story of the rise of the bourgeoisie to the dominant political and social position throughout the western world. It is the bourgeoisie that have given the modern period its distinctive commercial and industrial character. In 1500 commerce was still in a rudimentary stage, but it had advanced greatly in the preceding two centuries, and was on the eve of the "Commercial Revolution."

INDUSTRIAL DEVELOPMENT

Rise of Towns. The growth of the towns was one of the outstanding features of the later middle ages. The first strong impulses to commercial activity were given by the Crusades, which began late in the eleventh century. The Crusades stimulated travel and brought into western Europe new ideas, new luxuries, and new ways of living. Nothing so much tends to produce change in a society as such an influx of foreign civilization. The movement, once started, gathered momentum and weight like a rolling snowball. With increased trade, the city folk became more powerful. They threw off their feudal restrictions and had their privileges incorporated in a charter.

Early Towns. The towns of this period were small compared with modern ones. A population of 10,000 persons made a large city, and only a few great centers, such as Milan, Venice, London, and Paris had populations exceeding 100,000. Squalor and unsanitary conditions prevailed. There was no organized fire protection. The only police force was the "watch," proverbially inefficient and useless. Pigs, chickens, and other livestock routed in the mud of the narrow streets. A contemporary chronicler relates, without apparent astonishment, that wolves devoured fourteen persons in the heart of Paris in 1438. "Few venture to go alone in the country except in the middle of the day, and fewer still in the towns at night and least of all in London." So wrote a Venetian gentleman of the condition of England about 1497.

Merchant Gilds. The Merchant Gilds were organized in the eleventh century as a means of protection against feudal lords, thieves, and swindlers. Made up of all the merchants in the town, their functions were regulative, social, religious, and protective. By the sixteenth century they had declined, because of their failure to keep pace with the new industry and commerce. The dictatorial methods of the Merchant Gilds were responsible for the rise of the more democratic Craft Gilds.

Craft Gilds. The Craft Gilds, first organized in the thirteenth century, were composed of men in various industries. Each industry had its own gild. To these gilds is attributed the practice of serving first as an apprentice, then as a journeyman, in order to become a master workman. Regulation of membership, of methods and materials for manufacturing were the most important functions. Although continuing to exercise considerable power after the sixteenth century, the Gilds were losing the support of a new capitalist group that refused to abide by their regulations.

COMMERCIAL REVOLUTION

Growth of Commerce. Despite difficulties and hazards, commerce kept increasing during the late middle ages. Foremost in importance was the great luxury trade with the East. Spices and condiments, especially pepper, were much in demand in Europe to relieve the monotony of diet. From the East also came precious stones, fine textiles, rugs, and tapestries. In exchange for such products as these, Europe sent large quantities of coarse woolen cloth, and the raw metals tin, copper, and lead. But there remained what in modern times we should call an unfavorable balance of trade: Europe gradually drained herself of gold and silver to pay for her imported luxuries.

There were three main trade routes from the East — (1) the central route by way of the Persian Gulf, the Tigris valley, Bagdad, and Aleppo, (2) the southern route by way of the Red Sea, Cairo, and Alexandria, and (3) the northern route by way of Samarkand and Bokhara to the Black Sea. All these routes involved great difficulties and risks and many transfers of cargo.

Protection of Commerce. To protect their growing commerce from the attacks of robbers and pirates and from the extortions of feudal lords who demanded tolls for the right to travel, a number of the German commercial towns entered into a confederation known as the Hanseatic League. Formed in the thirteenth century, the Hanseatic League grew rapidly. At the height of its power and prestige more than seventy cities were members. The Hanseatic League maintained trading posts or "counters" in the principal Baltic and North Sea ports, made treaties providing for commercial privileges, and supported a fleet of ships for the suppression of piracy. In the fifteenth century the power of the Hanseatic League began to decline as its members found that its rules made competition with non-League cities difficult and as the causes that had led to its formation became less important. However, the League continued to function until the middle of the seventeenth century.

Impulse to Exploration. The lucrative trade with the East was, in the fifteenth century, largely the monopoly of the mercantile Italian cities, especially of Venice. This monopoly arose from the superiority of Venetian sea power in the Mediterranean and from the great length of time that the Italians had been engaged in the trade. They had built up their own organizations, routes, and trading-posts and had entered into commercial treaties with the Arabs and Turks. Early in the fifteenth century the possibility of discovering an all-water route to India began to be discussed in western Europe. Such a route would be of immense value since it would not only break the Venetian monopoly but would enable the saving of the expense of caravan transport and of the loading and unloading which the use of the old trade routes involved.

Advances in the science of navigation and in increasing knowledge of geography stimulated the spirit of exploration. The mariner's compass, invented in the thirteenth century, had come into general use by 1450 in spite of the prejudice that long prevailed against it as "an instrument evidently constructed by the devil." The astrolabe for measuring latitude came into use about the same time. The amazing account of the travels of Marco Polo (c. 1254 - c. 1324), who returned to Venice in 1295 after spending twenty years in the Far East and China, where he had lived at the court of Kublai, the Great Khan, stirred the imagination of educated Europe. Although fictional and full of extravagant tales, the very popular *Travels of Sir John Mandeville,* which appeared near the end of the fourteenth century, was probably even more influential than the factual *Book of Marco Polo* in stimulating interest in foreign lands. A famous passage in this latter book asserts as a generally known fact the roundness of the earth and declares that if one had ships and men, it would be possible to sail around the world and return to one's country. That the earth was round was known to a few learned men during the middle ages, but it was not until the fifteenth century that the knowledge was diffused at all widely.

It is no longer the opinion of historians that any substantial stimulus was given to the explorations of the late fifteenth century by the Turkish capture of Constantinople in 1453. It has been shown that the prices of spices and other articles of the East Indian trade did not rise perceptibly as a result of the fall of Constantinople and that the Venetian trade was carried on for many years with little interruption. It is also to be observed that the search for a new route to the East began many years before 1453 and that it was pressed not by the Venetians, with whose trade the Turks were presumably interfering, but by the Portuguese, Spanish, and English.

Rise of Portugal. The lead in oceanic exploration was taken by the Portuguese early in the fifteenth century. Under the direction of Prince Henry the Navigator (1394-1460) systematic exploration of the west coast of Africa and the adjacent Atlantic was carried out. Prince Henry attracted a group of learned men, adventurous mariners and astronomers, to his court at Sagres, and throughout his lifetime Portugal was the acknowledged center of geographic and maritime science. Prince Henry's captains discovered the Azores and Cape Verde Islands and pushed down the coast of Africa to the Gulf of Guinea. Whether or not Prince Henry ever entertained seriously the idea of reaching the Indies by sailing west — the idea that led Columbus to the discovery of America — there is no doubt that he believed that it should be possible to sail around Africa, and to the end of his life he was pushing expeditions to achieve this exploit. Nearly thirty years after Prince Henry's death the southernmost point of Africa was finally reached by the Portuguese Captain Bartholomew Diaz (1486). Twelve years later Prince Henry's dream was realized by Vasco da Gama, who sailed around the Cape of Good Hope, up the east coast of Africa, and across the Arabian Sea to India. By this voyage Da Gama destroyed at a blow the centuries old preëminence of Venice in the Eastern trade and raised his country for a time to the position of foremost commercial power in Europe.

Spain and the Discovery of America. In the meantime Spain had entered the field of competition for the eastern trade. It was partly the fame of the recent Portuguese discoveries and partly the desire to obtain similar glory for Spain that influenced Ferdinand and Isabella in their determination to furnish ships and men to the Italian adventurer, Christopher Columbus, who came to the Spanish court in 1484 with his scheme for reaching India by sailing directly west across the uncharted Atlantic. After delaying and negotiating for eight years, Columbus was furnished with three small vessels in 1492. He left Palos on August 3. Seventy days later he landed on a small island of the Bahama group, generally identified with the modern Watling Island. On this first voyage he also discovered the large islands of Cuba and Haiti (called by Columbus Espanola or Little Spain).

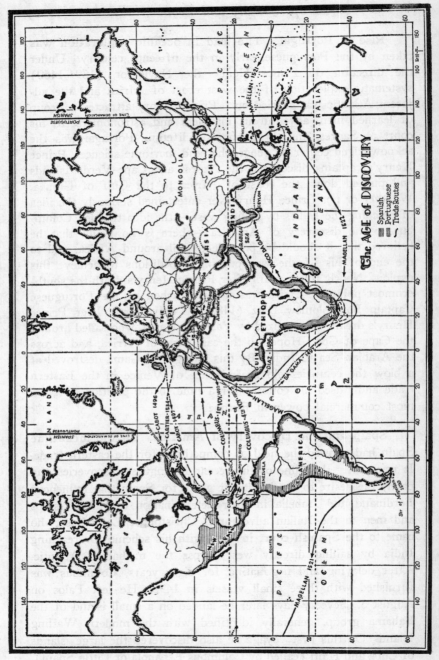

The Age of Discovery

Between 1493 and 1504 Columbus made three other voyages, discovered Puerto Rico, Jamaica, and many of the smaller West Indian islands, reached the mainland of South America near the mouth of the Orinoco, and explored the coast of Central America. The first white settlements in the New World were established by Columbus on the island of Haiti. Columbus never knew the real greatness of his discoveries. To the time of his death he believed he had reached the outposts of the East Indies.

In 1497 John Cabot, a Venetian navigator in the employ of Henry VII of England, sailed from Bristol and discovered Cape Breton Island, at the entrance to the Gulf of Saint Lawrence. In the following year he made a much more extended voyage, explored the southern tip of Greenland, reached the North American mainland coast of Labrador, sailed south around Newfoundland, and coasted the eastern shore of the United States as far south as Chesapeake Bay. Cabot, like Columbus, was seeking the East Indies.

Slowly the fact that no India, but a New World, had been opened up by these brave explorers began to dawn on the mind of Europe. The true character of this New World and a rough idea of its size were finally obtained in 1519-1522 when the ships of Ferdinand Magellan sailed through the straits at the extremity of South America, and then for more than three months ploughed across the vast Pacific. Magellan himself was killed in an encounter with the natives of the Philippine Islands, but the expedition continued, reached the East Indian islands, and returned to Spain across the Indian Ocean and by the known route of Vasco da Gama. Only one ship of the original five made the complete voyage. This was the first circumnavigation of the globe.

Period of Colonization. Between 1500 and 1550 a veritable army of explorers crossed the Atlantic, and discoveries came thick and fast. Greed, patriotism, the spirit of adventure, and religious zeal were mixed in about equal proportions as motives for this great exploring movement. Notable were Balboa's discovery of the Pacific (1513), Cortez' conquest of Mexico (1519-1521), Pizzaro's exploration and conquest of Peru (1531-1541), Cartier's voyages up the Saint Lawrence River (1534-1536),

De Soto's penetration of the North American continent to the Mississippi (1539-1542), and Francisco de Coronado's march north from Mexico into the regions of southwestern United States (1540). Following these pioneer expeditions, as the realization dawned of the immensity of the new regions, there came a long period of European colonization and the consequent spreading of European trade and civilization to a world-wide stage. During the sixteenth century the Portuguese and Spanish remained far in the lead in this scramble for colonies and trade (in 1493 Pope Alexander VI issued a famous bull dividing the entire New World between the Spanish and Portuguese); after the sixteenth century Spain and Portugal steadily declined in power and importance, while the Dutch, French, and English rose to be the great maritime powers of Europe.

PORTUGUESE COLONIAL EMPIRE. Vasco da Gama's discovery of the all-water route to India opened up a period of Portuguese expansion. War fleets as well as merchant ships were sent to the East, and within a few years the Portuguese had made themselves masters of several important ports, and by right of discovery they laid claim to all of Africa, southern Asia, and Brazil. However, circumstances prevented Portugal from defending her new territiories. The annexation of Portugal by Spain in 1580 and the closing of the port of Lisbon left some of her colonial empire to the mercy of the Dutch. Holland gained control of the East Indies, but Portugal was able to keep Brazil and other colonies.

SPANISH COLONIAL EMPIRE. At first the Spanish failed to find the desired riches in America, but the opening of Mexico by Hernando Cortez in 1519 and of Peru by Pizzaro in 1531 opened the treasure vaults. At first Spain profited from this new wealth and power. Later, however, she neglected the fundamentals of a healthy society and allowed trade and industry to decline. The Netherlands, a source of great wealth to Spain, revolted in 1566 and succeeded in throwing off the Spanish yoke. After this, Spain gradually lost possession after possession, while vigorous rivals pushed ahead.

RISE OF THE DUTCH AS COLONIZERS. As a result of the union of Spain and Portugal in 1580 and the revolt of the

Netherlands, the Dutch steadily rose to power, succeeding to the Portuguese Empire. Throughout the seventeenth century they monopolized the trade with Asia.

FRENCH AND ENGLISH. The French entered early the competition for colonial empire. French fishermen began to work the Grand Banks off Newfoundland within ten years of the discovery of America. But there was little colonization of the new regions until the beginning of the seventeenth century, when the French began extensive settlement in Canada. In 1562-1564 there had been attempts to found a Huguenot colony in Florida, but they were destroyed by the Spanish.

English exploration languished for more than half a century after the pioneer voyages of John Cabot. But upon the accession of Queen Elizabeth (1558) patriotic hatred of Spain and of Roman Catholicism was added to the motives of greed and adventure, and English sea-rovers such as John Hawkins and Francis Drake began to pillage Spanish commerce and lay the foundations of England's future maritime greatness. Hawkins discovered the immense profits to be made in the African slave trade. The explorers Frobisher (1576) and Davis (1585-87) sought the "Northwest Passage" to the Indies. The first English attempt at colonization in the New World was made in 1585 at Roanoke Island, Virginia, but the colony was apparently destroyed by the Indians about 1588. Not until 1607 was a permanent colony founded at Jamestown.

Results of the Commercial Revolution. The results of the Commercial Revolution were (1) the transfer of commerce from the Italian and German centers to the national states, (2) the instituting of a system called mercantilism, by which a favorable balance of trade would be obtained, (3) the formation of trading companies under charters, such as the regulated and the joint-stock company, (4) increased commerce resulting from new markets and new commodities, and (5) the rise of an increasingly powerful bourgeoisie who challenged the privileges of the old hereditary nobility, and who, by their energy, enterprise, and determination for political power, became the central driving-force for social change. In general, it Europeanized the world.

CHAPTER III.

EUROPE POLITICALLY IN THE SIXTEENTH CENTURY

CHARLES V AND PHILIP II DOMINATED SIXTEENTH CENTURY POLITICS

Charles V, Holy Roman Emperor (1519-1556). The leading figure in European politics during the first part of the sixteenth century was Charles of Hapsburg who combined into one of the greatest empires ever controlled by one man the Spanish territory of Ferdinand (1516) and, upon the death of Maximilian (1519), the Hapsburg dominion of Austria and the Netherlands. In 1519, too, he was crowned as Charles V of the Holy Roman Empire in spite of Francis I of France, who tried to gain the crown for himself. Among the problems confronting Charles V were (a) the Moors in Africa, (b) Moors and Turks in the Mediterranean, (c) trade and dynastic rivalry with France, (d) suffocation of Protestantism in Germany and elsewhere, and (e) the opposition of the nobility to his centralizing program.

WARS WITH FRANCE. The wars between Charles V and Francis I of France commenced in 1521. Territorial rivalry over the possession of Milan and Naples in Italy, of Navarre in Spain, of Burgundy and the French-speaking Netherlands, and personal rivalry over the contest for the crown of the Holy Roman Empire were the principal causes. A series of spasmodic outbreaks followed until the treaty of Cateau Cambrésis (1559), which gave the Hapsburgs control of most of Italy but allowed the French to extend their frontier towards the Rhine. These wars allowed (a) the Ottoman Empire to increase its power in Europe, (b) the Protestants to increase their power and prestige in Germany, and (c) the French to preserve "a balance of power" in Europe.

CONFLICT WITH THE TURKS. Under Suleiman II (1520-1566) the Turkish dominion had been extended until the whole eastern Mediterranean, with the exception of a few small islands, was a Moslem lake. In 1521 Suleiman II declared war on Hungary and completely overwhelmed the Hungarians at Mohács (1526). He attempted to conquer Austria, but the siege of Vienna (1529) failed. In 1547 Charles V was compelled to recognize the Turkish conquest of Hungary. Attempts of Charles V to oust the Turks were unsuccessful, and the Turks remained as a dark cloud upon the horizon of his dominions. Later Philip II of Spain helped greatly in saving Western Europe by furnishing men and equipment in the battle of Lepanto (1571), which checked the Ottoman advance.

DOMESTIC CONCERNS OF CHARLES V. The domestic concerns of Charles V were as great as his foreign ones. The desire to weld his heterogeneous empire into a united state was his great ambition. But he was unwilling to sacrifice the pretensions of the Holy Roman Empire to universal sovereignty, and thus he worked counter to the rising force of German nationalism. The Protestant Revolt, too, was a complicating factor. The nobility arrayed itself against the centralizing influence of the Emperor and his desire for increased power. The German knights were strongly nationalistic, but their attempts at consolidation were checked by the princes. The spread of Lutheranism and its acceptance by the knights precipitated a conflict (Knights' War, 1522-23) which definitely retarded national unity among the Germans.

Philip II and the Spanish Hapsburgs (1556-1598). In 1555-56 Charles V, weary of his complex responsibilities, abdicated his various crowns. His son Philip II obtained Spain, Netherlands, East Burgundy, and parts of Italy; his brother Ferdinand succeeded to his powers as Holy Roman Emperor and received the formal title on Charles' death in 1558. Philip dominated the age in which he lived, as his father had before him. The incidents during Philip's reign were grouped around his desire to crush out Protestantism and to make Spain supreme in the world. His failure to accomplish these ends may be attributed to the multiplicity of conflicting problems about him.

INTERNAL REFORMS IN SPAIN. In Spain Philip II sought further to unify the country, to improve its financial status, to strengthen Catholicism, and to drive out the Moors. He succeeded in joining Portugal with Spain (1580), but this union ended in 1640.

REVOLT OF THE NETHERLANDS. The revolt of the Netherlands was caused by (a) the increased taxes of Philip II, (b) his political errors, (c) his attempts to crush out Calvinistic Protestantism, and (d) his personal unpopularity. Attempts to pacify the nobles and burghers by granting minor concessions were made. Philip's promise to abolish the inquisition was revoked when a group of radicals began destroying the property of the Catholic churches. The Duke of Alva was sent to the Netherlands (1567-73) and he cruelly tried to crush Philip's opponents. The Duke's harsh laws and increased taxation served to unite the Southern and Northern Netherlands against Philip. The leader of the opposition was William the Silent of Orange (1533-1584), who constantly harassed Alva by land and sea. Alva was replaced by Requesens, who was even less successful. Upon the death of Requesens, the Spanish army, without a leader, pay, or food, pillaged several cities (Spanish Fury, 1576). This led to the "Pacification of Ghent," by which the people of the Netherlands vowed resistance to the obnoxious laws imposed upon them.

TREATIES OF ARRAS AND OF UTRECHT. Alexander Farnese became governor and effected a treaty at Arras (1579) guaranteeing protection for the Catholic religion in the Southern Provinces, and leading to a reunion of these provinces (roughly modern Belgium) with the Spanish crown. The Northern Provinces, on the other hand, signed the Union of Utrecht, a manifesto of resistance to Spanish tyranny. The Southern part (Spanish or Austrian Netherlands) remained a part of the Hapsburg dominions for two centuries, but the Northern (Holland) under William the Silent continued to frustrate subjugation and declared its independence in 1581 (Act of Abjuration). Spain refused to recognize Dutch independence until the treaty of Westphalia, in 1648.

PHILIP II AND ENGLAND. In 1554 Philip married Mary Tudor, Queen of England. But he was not popular with the English, and he shared the general obloquy that followed Mary's attempt to reëstablish Roman Catholicism in England. The accession of Elizabeth (1558) destroyed Philip's influence in England. When Elizabeth did not accept Philip's proposal for marriage, he tried to stir up the English against their Protestant Queen. The Catholic, Mary Stuart, Queen of Scotland, was the tool for many futile attempts to obtain power in England. The beheading of Mary by Elizabeth in 1587 gave Philip II provocation for armed intervention. The Great Armada set sail from Spain (1588) only to be defeated by Englishmen and the elements. Philip thus failed to recover his influence over England, and worse, Spain gradually lost her commercial supremacy to England.

France in the Second Half of the Sixteenth Century. The successor of Francis I on the French throne was Henry II (1547-59). He maintained a tyrannical government and severely persecuted the growing sect of Huguenots (Protestants). During his reign a powerful family, the Guises, gained great influence. The Guises championed the Catholic Church. After Henry's death a second powerful family, the Bourbons, became rivals of the Guises and allies of the Huguenots. The ambitious Catherine de' Medici, widow of Henry II, and the chief power behind the throne during the reign of her weak son Charles IX (1560-74), tried to steer a middle course between the rivals and take advantage of their quarrels for her son's aggrandizement. The strife of various factions, complicated by both political and religious issues, resulted in a series of civil wars that kept the nation in an uproar. In 1572 the massacre of Saint Bartholomew's Day occurred. It was ordered by Charles IX at the instance of Catherine, who feared that the Huguenots, led by the able Admiral Coligny, had become too powerful. Thousands of Huguenots were killed, but the strife of faction continued. A party known as the "Politiques" arose favoring religious toleration and the ending of the bloody and costly civil wars.

By 1585 it had become evident that there would be no direct male successor to Henry III (1574-1589), the last of Catherine de' Medici's sons, and that the crown would accordingly pass to the Bourbon Henry of Navarre. Henry of Navarre was a Protestant, and the prospect of his accession was distasteful not only to the Guise family but to Philip II of Spain. Henry of Guise accordingly allied himself with Philip and attempted to seize the throne. Thus was precipitated a conflict known as the War of the Three Henries. In 1588 Henry of Guise was assassinated, and in 1589 the same fate overtook Henry III. Henry of Navaree was left without a strong personal rival for the throne, and Philip of Spain, weakened by his war with England and by internal difficulties, was unable to prevent the triumph of his enemy. For several years Henry of Navarre (Henry IV of France) continued to be opposed by the Guise party, but in 1593, with his acceptance of Catholicism, the religious opposition to him waned, and in 1598 the long struggle came to an end with Henry's issuance of the famous Edict of Nantes, which granted the Huguenots a limited freedom of worship and political equality with Catholics. "We do establish and proclaim . . . that the recollection of everything done by one party or the other between March, 1585, and our accession to the crown, and during all the preceding period of troubles, remain obliterated and forgotten as if no such things had ever happened." However, in 1610 Henry IV, like Henry of Guise and Henry III, was the victim of an assassin.

┌─────────────────────────────────┐
│ *Significant Dates*   │
│   │
│ Christian Church Separates . 1054 │
│ Luther's Theses Published . 1517 │
│ Henry VIII Breaks with   │
│   Church . . . . 1534 │
│ Founding of the Jesuits . . 1534 │
│ Edict of Nantes . . . . . 1598 │
└─────────────────────────────────┘

CHAPTER IV.

EUROPE RELIGIOUSLY IN THE SIXTEENTH CENTURY

THE CATHOLIC CHURCH IN 1500

The Church Universal. At the beginning of the sixteenth century the sole religious organization of Western Europe was the Roman Catholic Church. It differed from modern religious bodies in that it claimed membership, financial support, and obedience from all. It was intimately associated with the secular government, which undertook to enforce the Church's claim of authority. Failure to observe the discipline of the Church, or attacks on its dogma were regarded as crimes against the State.

Organization of the Catholic Church. The Church functioned through a vast hierarchy of clergy. The Bishop of Rome was at the head of the Mother Church, having been elected Pope for life by a group of Cardinals. The local administration was cared for by sub-dividing the Catholic world into (1) patriarchates, (2) provinces, (3) dioceses, and (4) parishes. The officers of this organization were termed "Secular" clergy. The "regular" clergy were the monks who renounced the world and lived by set rules. Some lived in fixed homes—Benedictine monks; others went on crusades and bore arms—Knights Templars; still others

25

wandered around preaching to the people—Franciscans and Dominicans. From time to time general councils—assemblies of prelates representing the whole Church—met for the discussion of Church legislation, or to iron out some problem of dogma or organization. Early in the fifteenth century there was a movement to invest these general councils with supreme authority within the Church, but after the Council of Ferrara-Florence (1438-1443), the Pope was recognized as superior to a general council. The Pope was the supreme law-giver, supreme judge, and supreme administrator in church matters. He claimed certain temporal powers such as the right to crown the Holy Roman Emperor, depose a ruler, declare a law void, rule over Rome, and to lay taxes throughout the Catholic world.

Mission of the Catholic Church. The mission of the Catholic Church was the salvation of souls for eternity through the teachings of Jesus Christ. The dogmas and faith of the Catholic Church make up its theology, the center of which is the sacramental system, the only means of saving souls. The seven sacraments are baptism, confirmation, Holy Eucharist, penance, extreme unction, holy orders, and matrimony. The priesthood was the indispensable agent of the Church in administering many of the sacraments to the people.

Opposition to the Catholic Church. The Church reached the height of its temporal power and prestige in the thirteenth century. During the fourteenth and fifteenth centuries, with the rise of the national monarchies, the increase of independent thinking, and a moral decline within the Church itself, considerable opposition developed.

NEW NATIONAL STATES. Opposition to the Church was especially evident in the new national states of western Europe. The clergy and the monarchs debated over the power (a) to appoint high church officers, (b) to tax church property, (c) to have cases tried in ecclesiastical courts instead of state courts, and (d) of the Pope to interfere in state matters. A series of conflicts occurred from the twelfth century on, and a number of anti-papal laws were enacted, but they were poorly enforced, and the Pope was still supreme in the affairs of church government in 1500.

DISUNITY OF THE CHURCH. The development of a great Christian schism and the rise of Mohammedanism served to disunite Catholicism. The Eastern or Greek Orthodox Church separated from the Roman Church in 1054 over minor differences in dogmas and has never reunited. Mohammedanism spread over western Asia, northern Africa, even to far-away Spain and eastern Europe, threatening the growth and development of Catholic Christianity. Less important, but factors for concern, were the heretics such as John Wycliffe and John Huss, and the skeptics, who outwardly accepted Catholicism but either disagreed with its dogma or doubted its value.

PROTESTANT REVOLT

Causes for Protestant Revolt. The causes for the breaking away of a group from the Catholic Church were (1) the continued conflict between spiritual and temporal powers which was brought to a head by nationalism, (2) the great wealth of the Catholic Church and its heavy taxes upon the common people, (3) the presence of certain abuses in the Catholic Church such as immorality, simony, and nepotism, and (4) the growth of a new spirit of religious piety.

New Theology. The objections to Catholicism of such humanists as Erasmus gave impetus to a new theology which progressed tremendously under men like Luther, Calvin, Knox, and Zwingli. The teachings of Huss and Wycliffe offered the foundations for the new ideas. Characteristic of the new theology was its emphasis on the personal spiritual regeneration of the individual and rejection of the formulas of the church.

But the humanist movement furthered the rise of Protestantism chiefly through the humanist attacks on abuses in the Catholic Church. The Protestant leaders were not the inheritors of the humanistic tradition of tolerance and free intellectual inquiry.

Lutheranism. The Protestant Revolt took place in Germany, Scandinavia, Poland, Dutch Netherlands, Switzerland, Scotland, England, Bohemia, and parts of Hungary. One form of Protestant Christianity was Lutheranism, which took its name from the founder, Martin Luther and originated in Germany and Scandinavia.

MARTIN LUTHER. Luther's theology was based on the idea of "justification by faith" in opposition to the Church's doctrine of "justification by sacraments and works." The sale of indulgences by Tetzel prompted Luther to publish his Ninety-Five Theses (Wittenberg, 1517), espousing the idea of "salvation through faith." In the debate at Leipzig between Luther and John Eck, Luther was forced into admissions identical with the views of John Huss which views had been condemned as heretical by the Council of Constance (1414-1418). Up to this time Luther had not regarded himself as a heretic but as a reformer from within. He now saw that he must either recant his conclusions or begin an open war against the whole church system. He chose the latter course, and in 1520 issued three powerful pamphlets attacking the church on both political and theological grounds. The Pope excommunicated him the following year (1521). The new theology appealed to simple and pious people because of its spiritual fervor; to the materialists, who were glad of an opportunity to seize the rich church property; and to the patriots, who regarded the Pope as an obstacle to German national unity. Its spread over Germany was further fostered both by the personality of its founder and by the laxity of Charles V in domestic matters while he was striving to prevent foreign aggression.

SIGNIFICANCE OF THE PEASANTS' REVOLT. The peasants proceeded to accept Luther's challenge to the princes to seize church lands and correct abuses. Luther did not object as long as the Peasants' Revolt was aimed against the Catholic Church, but when it was directed against the new Lutheran nobles, he sided with the nobles and helped to crush the revolt (1525), because he needed the support of the nobles to spread his own theology. As a result, the nobles became more powerful than ever, and Luther lost the support of the peasants.

LUTHERANISM ACCEPTED IN THE NORTHERN GERMANIES. The Diet of Speyer (1526) at first failed to condemn Lutheranism but later (1529) condemned it as a heresy. A legal protest was made by the Lutheran princes, hence the name *Protestant*. The Confession of Augsburg (1530) constitutes the Lutheran Creed. The next few years were filled with religious conflicts, but these ended in 1555 with the Peace of Augsburg, which provided that (a) each prince would decide the religion for his sub-jects, (b) Protestants could keep church property acquired before 1552, (c) Lutheranism was the only form of Protestantism allówed, (d) Lutherans living in ecclesiastical states could keep their faith, and (e) ecclesiastical princes becoming Protestants were to give up their sees. Thus Lutheranism had won acceptance in the Northern Germanies.

LUTHERANISM IN DENMARK AND SWEDEN. Lutheranism was established in the Scandinavian countries chiefly as a result of the efforts of the kings, Frederick I of Denmark and Norway (1523-1533) and Gustavus Vasa of Sweden (1523-1560). These kings saw in the new church an opportunity to solidify their political control. In Denmark and Norway Frederick I encouraged Lutheran teaching and by 1527 he had Lutheranism on a par with Catholicism. When Christian III succeeded him in 1536, after a popular uprising by the Catholics had failed, Lutheranism triumphed and was made the state religion (1537). In Sweden, King Gustavus Vasa was led to renounce Catholicism, and by 1593 Lutheranism was the religion of Sweden. Catholics were later deprived of offices and estates, and were banished from the kingdom (1604).

NON-RELIGIOUS CAUSES FOR LUTHER'S SUCCESS. The Lutheran Revolt would have been no more successful than the similar movements of Wycliffe and Huss had not a number of essentially non-religious factors worked in its favor. First among these was the determination of the German princes to secure greater independence for themselves and to stop the diversion of revenue from their own coffers to the papal court. From the very first Luther had the support of such powerful men as Frederick the Wise, Elector of Saxony; of his brother John; of Philip, Landgrave of Hesse; and of the leaders of the free commercial cities. These men were probably motivated more by patriotic and economic considerations than by religious enthusi-asm. The opportunity offered by the Protestant Revolt for the seizure of rich church lands made many of the princes zealous for the cause though they cared little for the theological points involved.

The national and patriotic element was also of great importance. German patriots looked upon the papacy as a foreign secular power to which Germany was enslaved. Such men as the Knights Franz von Sickengen and Ulrich von Hutten were little interested in religion but were intensely indignant that an Italian potentate should be able to dictate to free Germans and that large sums of money should be drained out of Germany "to support in idle indulgence in Rome a vast number of the worst of men." In his *Address to the Christian Nobility of the German Nation,* Luther himself appealed strongly to German patriotism, stressing the shame of German serfage to Rome and calling upon the princes to rally around the newly-elected emperor. However, the Emperor Charles V remained to the last both a stanch Catholic and a traditional imperialist, so that actually the Protestant movement, by setting the princes, the religious leaders, and the emperor at odds, tended to destroy whatever basis for a national state may have existed.

During the critical period of the rise of German Protestantism (1520-1546), Charles V and his brother Ferdinand were so harassed by foreign complications—wars with Francis I of France and with the Ottoman Turks, administrative difficulties in Spain and the Netherlands, disagreements with the Pope—that they were never able to devote themselves wholeheartedly to suppressing the religious revolt. It must also be added that Charles V, though zealous to reëstablish Roman Catholic uniformity throughout his dominions, was by no means a cruel and uncompromising bigot, and on many occasions pursued a course of remarkable moderation. It would have been quite in accord with the contemporary spirit had Charles put down the Protestant movement in its early stages with rope and fagot, as he was actually urged to do by the extreme party at the Diet of Worms; instead he tried throughout his life to conciliate his opponents and to effect his ends with as little bloodshed as possible.

Calvinism. The type of Protestantism which was the basis for the modern Presbyterian, Congregational, and Reformed Churches was Calvinism.

HULDREICH ZWINGLI. In Switzerland Huldreich Zwingli started to oppose the Roman church, and from the cathedral at

Zürich he attacked the old dogmas. Zürich replied to a papal appeal (1523) to remove Zwingli by declaring its independence from Catholicism. An attempt to make the whole of Switzerland Protestant failed. The five forest cantons remained Catholic. In 1529 a notable attempt was made by the young Lutheran Prince, Philip of Hesse, to bring about a union between Luther and Zwingli. The two leaders met but could not agree on the doctrine of the Eucharist. Henceforth Protestantism remained separated and developed more and more along sectarian lines.

JOHN CALVIN. The death of Zwingli (1531) left the new Swiss Protestantism without a leader until the appearance of John Calvin at Geneva in 1536. While at Basel, Switzerland, he wrote *The Institutes of the Christian Religion* (1536) revealing the germ of the new Calvinism which was part Lutheran and part Zwinglian. It failed to unite Protestantism, however, because of the wide differences between Luther and Calvin. At Geneva Calvin as political and religious leader set the example of Protestantism for his disciples throughout Europe and kept in touch with them by writing treatises and letters. Calvin easily succeeded Zwingli in Switzerland as the religious leader. The French did not accept Protestantism so readily nor so completely as some other countries. The main support of Calvin in France came from the middle class. Civil conflicts ended in the Edict of Nantes (1598), which promised religious freedom to Calvinists without loss of political rights. In the struggle with Spain the Southern Netherlands remained Catholic, while the Northern were able to throw off the Spanish yoke and accept Calvinism in place of Lutheranism, which had been stamped out by Charles V. In Southern Germany Calvinism gained headway with the peasants, but it was greatly handicapped by the treaty of Augsburg (1555), which recognized only Lutheranism as a form of Protestantism in Germany. Calvinism in Scotland was fostered by John Knox and by the desire of many to reform the Catholic Church. After spending a few years with Calvin, Knox returned to Scotland and in a political and religious coup made Calvinism supreme. Even in England Calvinism influenced the Anglican Church and under Oliver Cromwell in the seventeenth century it had a temporary triumph. After 1689 a measure of religious toleration was granted to the Calvinistic sects of England.

Anglicanism. A third branch of Protestantism was Anglicanism, of which the Episcopal Church in the United States and the Established Church of England are the modern outgrowths. Anglicanism is the most conservative form of Protestantism, being essentially the old Roman Catholic Church of England modified somewhat and separated from the Pope and his hierarchy.

CAUSES FOR OPPOSITION TO THE CATHOLIC CHURCH IN ENGLAND. The reasons for opposition to the Catholic Church were (a) the need for reform in morals and manners, (b) the spreading of Lutheran propaganda which started people thinking, (c) the exercise of temporal power by the Pope, and (d) the increased power of the King of England. Henry VIII (1509-1547) at first tried to crush Lutheranism and to support the Pope. But the attempt of Henry VIII to get rid of his wife, Catherine, so that he might marry Anne Boleyn caused friction with the Pope. Henry further antagonized the Catholic clergy, made himself head of the church, and appointed Thomas Cranmer Archbishop of Canterbury. Cranmer immediately declared the marriage with Catherine null and void and sanctioned the union with Anne Boleyn. After this, the Pope, Clement VII, handed down a decision favorable to Catherine and excommunicated Henry VIII. However, Henry VIII had parliament pass a series of laws which made him the ecclesiastical head of the Church of England (1534). The attempt of the Lutherans to make England Protestant failed when Henry VIII published the Six Articles, which reaffirmed the Catholic beliefs but placed the king at the head of the church, instead of the Pope. Both Catholics and Protestants were persecuted by Henry VIII. The monasteries were confiscated and sold not only for religious reasons but also to provide Henry with funds.

PERMANENCE OF THE WORK OF ELIZABETH. During the reign of the young Edward VI (1547-1553) there was a considerable movement away from Henry VIII's "Popery without the Pope." In 1552 and 1553, with the issuance of the *Second Book of Common Prayer* and the Forty-Two Articles of faith, the essential body of Anglican doctrine was established. Anglicanism accepted the characteristic Protestant doctrines denying transubstantiation and insisting upon justification by faith and on the supremacy of the Scriptures as the rule of faith but preserved much of the ritual of the old religion. Mary Tudor (1553-1558) undid the work of Henry VIII and Edward VI and restored Catholicism to England. However, Mary was not able to blot Protestantism out but only to curb it for a while. The marriage of Mary to Philip II of Spain did not produce an heir, and Elizabeth, daughter of Anne Boleyn, became Queen. Elizabeth was a Protestant and under her the Anglican Church took final shape. The Forty-Two Articles of faith were consolidated into the Thirty-Nine Articles. Elizabeth appointed bishops that would accept the new theology, and harsh laws were imposed upon non-conformists.

CATHOLIC COUNTER-REFORMATION

The movement of separation from the Catholic Church was long known in Protestant countries as the "Reformation." It is more accurate to call it the Protestant Revolt and to reserve the term "Reformation" or "Counter-Reformation" for the movement within the Catholic Church that followed the Protestant Revolt and corrected many of the abuses that had been partly responsible for the Protestant Revolt.

Pope Paul III and Nepotism. The practice of the Popes of bestowing offices upon relatives (nepotism) was brought to an end by Paul III (1534-1549), who appointed church officers for their virtue and learning.

Reforms at the Council of Trent (1545-1563). A second part of the Catholic Counter-Reformation was the dogmatic and reformatory work of the Council of Trent (1545-1563). Refusing to compromise on theological questions with the Protestants, the Catholic representatives at Trent supported the old dogmas. But many abuses of practice were censured — sale of church offices condemned, issuance of indulgences for money prohibited, and worldly pursuits by bishops abolished. An Index was prepared, listing dangerous and heretical books which Catholics should not read, and the ecclesiastical court of the Inquisition was given power to punish delinquents for lapses of faith and conduct.

New Religious Societies. Several new religious societies were formed which sought to purify the life of the people. The most important was the Society of Jesus, the Jesuits, founded by Ignatius Loyola in 1534. The Jesuits sought to win back the lost prestige of the Catholic Church. As missionaries they went out and won back Poland and Bavaria from Lutheranism. They went into Asia and America to win converts to the Pope of Rome. Their skill as teachers and propagandists, developed by a long and rigorous training, together with their single-minded devotion to their leader and their religion, made them a most powerful force in the regeneration of the Catholic Church after the shattering blow of the Protestant Revolt.

Catholic Countries. The Catholic countries of Italy, Spain, Portugal, Austria, and Ireland remained firm in their allegiance to Catholicism. In France Protestantism made considerable headway but did not become the dominant religion. The causes for dissatisfaction were corrected, and the royal powers found strength in the Catholic Church.

RESULTS OF THE PROTESTANT REVOLT

Religious Results. There were various manifestations of the far-reaching results of the Protestant Revolt — (1) The Catholic Church was broken up by the great revolt against the old order. (2) Individual morality and theological study were encouraged. (3) The Christian religion became largely nationalized. (4) The Roman Catholic dogma was considerably narrowed by a continued defensive attitude toward the Protestants.

Social and Political Changes. Important political and social changes resulted, which affected all classes. Most obvious was the great loss of the temporal power of the Pope with a corresponding increase in the powers of the national governments. No longer was there a universal organization able to claim superiority over all kings and potentates. A second result was the injection of the religious issue into domestic and international politics. For more than a hundred years (1546-1648) Europe was distracted by a series of international and civil wars in practically all of which the religious issue was prominent.

Intellectual and Cultural Results. Intellectually, Protestantism was a religious revival, not a rationalist movement. Its first effects did not result in a new spirit of religious tolerance. In those countries where Protestantism was strongest, popular education under state control became more and more common. But within the Catholic Church the growing movement of humanism that had found expression in the urbane scholarship of such men as Erasmus and Thomas More was stifled. But the multiplication of sects that began with the Protestant Revolt resulted in the long run in the spread of tolerance, if only because it was seen to be impossible to enforce uniformity of faith in a large community.

CHAPTER V.

EUROPE CULTURALLY IN THE SIXTEENTH CENTURY

ANCIENT AND MEDIEVAL CULTURE

Contributions of the Greeks and Romans. Centuries before this period the early Greeks created the first complex and mature culture. In poetry and drama, in philosophy, and in sculpture and architecture they produced masterpieces that have never been surpassed. In science and mathematics they laid a magnificent groundwork. Likewise the early Romans, though much less original and versatile than the Greeks, created a great Latin literature based on Greek models, and made substantial contributions of their own to architecture and engineering. But their most valuable gift to civilization was their system of government and law and their development of a great empire that was the means of preserving the treasures of ancient culture.

Contributions of the Mohammedans. The Mohammedans brought many of the Eastern contributions to culture to the West. From Asia they borrowed algebra, arabic numerals, the compass, and the method of weaving rich rugs and tapestries. Their great contributions were in the realm of useful knowledge and their secular outlook.

Characteristics of Medieval Culture. Medieval culture was inspired by Christianity and the Catholic Church. The contributions of the Greeks, Romans, and Moslems must be recognized also. In the twelfth and thirteenth centuries a remarkable flowering of culture occurred. From this period date the subtle scholastic philosophy, the great Gothic cathedrals, the foundations of the universities, and the beginnings of a revived experimental science.

INVENTION OF PRINTING

Development of Paper. Various materials have been used for writing since early times. The ancient Assyrians used clay bricks or cylinders. The Egyptians and later the Greeks and Romans used sheets made from the papyrus plant. In the middle ages the usual material was parchment or dressed skin. Before printing could develop on a large scale, it was necessary to find a material much cheaper than parchment. The problem was solved with the development of paper.

Movable Type. The evolution of movable type was a slow process. The insignia of early rulers came first, then the block system, and finally the movable type.

Early Printing Presses. The first printed matter from the presses utilizing movable type were a Bible and some papal letters in 1454. By 1466 printing presses were erected in Rome, and by the sixteenth century book publishers were found in every large city. As a result of this invention (1) the number of books increased greatly, (2) the demand increased as the price of books decreased, and (3) a greater degree of accuracy was assured.

HUMANISM

The movement known as humanism arose in the fourteenth and fifteenth centuries. In its narrow sense humanism meant a revival of study of the Greek and Latin classics. In a broader sense humanism meant the turning away from the medieval traditions of asceticism and preoccupation with theology toward interest in man's life on this earth. Critical point of view toward literature helped to promote a search for new bases of facts. In this sense humanism was the parent of modern cultural and scientific development.

Petrarch (1304-1374). The first great humanist was Francesco Petrarch (Petrarch 1304-1374). Petrarch felt the pleasure of mere human life — the "joy of living, a confidence in human ability and power, and a sympathetic understanding with the past." This was the basis of humanism, which spread out and reached its greatest height in Italy.

Erasmus (1466-1536). In the sixteenth century the leader of humanism was Erasmus (1466-1536), an outstanding European scholar. Erasmus disapproved of rebelling against the Catholic Church, and the leading humanist remained Catholic. Humanism has declined as an independent intellectual interest, but it still lives in higher education and in the historical "humanities"— Latin, Greek, and history as taught in college and high school.

ART IN THE SIXTEENTH CENTURY

Sixteenth century art represented a combination of new ideas with the classical simplicity of the Greeks and Romans. This new spirit is one of the bases of modern art.

Architecture. The new architecture used the old Greek columns — Doric, Ionic, and Corinthian — and had the plain and straight lines of Greek temples or the graceful curve of the Roman dome. Getting its start in Italy, the new architecture spread to France, Spain, and later to England.

Sculpture. The sculpture of this period combined the old and new, although in the fifteenth century under Ghiberti and Donatello the Greek and Roman influences predominated. Michelangelo greatly enlarged the possibilities of sculpture. Like architecture, the new sculpture spread from Italy throughout Europe.

Modern Painting. Modern painting released itself from the classical style to a greater extent than any of the other arts. In the hands of such masters as Leonardo da Vinci, Michelangelo, Raphael, and Titian, it reached a high degree of perfection in sixteenth century Italy.

LEONARDO DA VINCI. Leonardo da Vinci (1452-1519), a Florentine artist, engineer, architect, scientist, and mathematician, is noted for his great paintings, *Mona Lisa* and *The Last Supper,* because of their mysterious beauty obtained through his masterful use of perspective, light, shade, and color.

MICHELANGELO. Michelangelo (1475-1564), also a Florentine, was a great painter and sculptor and a poet. His work on St. Peter's Cathedral at Rome and in the Sistine Chapel are enduring monuments to his genius.

RAPHAEL. Raphael (1483-1520) is considered one of the greatest painters, having the ability to obtain harmonious composition and linear beauty without losing grace or charm in his works. He spent considerable time decorating the Vatican palace.

TITIAN. Titian (1477-1576), a Venetian, is noted for his harmony of light and color, using the bright hues of the Venetians. His portrait of Philip II and his painting of the Council of Trent are among his best known works.

OTHER PAINTERS. The artistic richness of the period which spread from Italy may be indicated by the mere citation of the names of such artists as Alessandro Botticelli (c. 1447-1510), Albrecht Dürer (1471-1528), Sebastian del Piombo (1485-1547), Andrea del Sarto (1486-1531), Hans Holbein (1497-1543), and Antonio da Corregio (1494-1534).

Music. Great advances in the field of music were made during this period, especially in the development of instruments, among them the new violin and the forerunner of our piano, the harpsichord. The first of the great modern composers was the Frenchman Josquin Des Prés (c. 1450-1521). Known as the "Prince of Music" Josquin showed a finished mastery that justifies regarding him as the father of modern composition. Best known of all the sixteenth century composers, however, was Palestrina (1524-1594), a papal organist, whose severe and simple style commended him to the Council of Trent. His influence is still great in the Catholic Church.

DEVELOPMENT OF NATIONAL LITERATURE

National Literatures. Latin had been the universal language of culture during the middle ages, and its position was further strengthened by the humanists. But the sixteenth century, with its nationalistic tendencies, its social, political and religious unrest, demanded separate literatures — a national literature for Italians, Frenchmen, Spaniards, Germans, Englishmen, and others.

DEVELOPMENT OF THE ITALIAN LITERATURE. As in other phases of culture, Italy was a leader in establishing a national literature. A great national literature was created in the fourteenth century by Dante, Boccaccio, and Petrarch. The tradition was ably carried on in the fifteenth and sixteenth centuries by Niccolò Machiavelli (1469-1527), historian and political philosopher, Ludovico Ariosto (1474-1533), the poet, Torquato Tasso (1544-1595), and many others.

FRENCH LITERATURE. Under Francis I, French literature received an impetus, but it did not reach its height until the next century. François Rabelais (1490-1553) was the most famous French author of this period. In the second half of the sixteenth century the greatest name was that of Michel de Montaigne (1533-1592), whose *Essays* are pervaded by the urbane, skeptical, tolerant spirit of humanism.

CERVANTES AND THE SPANISH LITERATURE. Cervantes' *Don Quixote* (published 1605) was Spain's worthy contribution to the new national literature of Europe. Lope de Vega (1562-1635) was a dramatist of astonishing productiveness; he is believed to have written more than 1,000 plays.

MARTIN LUTHER AND THE GERMAN LITERATURE. Martin Luther in Germany encouraged a national literature when he printed his Bible in German.

GOLDEN AGE OF LITERATURE IN ENGLAND. English literature of the late sixteenth and early seventeenth centuries was at its height with such writers as Edmund Spenser, William Shakespeare, Francis Bacon, Ben Jonson, Richard Hooker, and later, John Milton.

PROGRESS IN SCIENCE

The beginnings of modern experimental and natural science reveal the progress made in reasoning. The sixteenth and seventeenth centuries saw an immense development in science. Among the causes may be noted (1) the recovery and more enlightened study of Greek, Roman, and Moslem scientific information, (2) the invention of printing and the diffusion of knowledge, (3) the discoveries of new trade routes that increased geographical knowledge, and (4) the work of Francis Bacon and René Descartes in developing a method for the new science.

Work of Copernicus, Kepler, and Galileo. Medieval astronomy was largely used as a means of foretelling the future (astrology). But although this practice was still popular in the sixteenth century, the scientific study of the stars had never entirely died out and was pursued by an increasing number of men during the fourteenth and fifteenth centuries. In 1543 the publication of Nicolaus Copernicus' *Revolutions of the Celestial Bodies* heralded a complete overturn in astronomical theory. Copernicus (1473-1543) discarded the Ptolemaic theory that the earth was the center of the universe and proposed the Copernican system which fixes the earth as one of the many planets which revolve around the sun. Johann Kepler (1571-1630), a German, further developed Copernicus' theory, and Galileo (1564-1642), an Italian, brought it to the attention of learned men and popularized it.

Gregorian Calendar (1582). Pope Gregory XIII (1572-1585) took advantage of the liberalizing influences of the period and of other factors upon sixteenth century thinking to correct some of the weaknesses of the Julian calendar. The calendar was advanced ten days, and leap years were omitted in each century year, except where divisible by four hundred. The new calendar was immediately accepted by Catholic countries and later by other nations.

Inductive and Deductive Reasoning. Most early science used the deductive method of reasoning — proceeding from the general to the specific. The scholastic philosophers of the thirteenth and fourteenth centuries, basing their work on the logic of Aristotle, developed deductive reasoning. This method, however, did not help to broaden or develop science to any great extent. But when Francis Bacon popularized the inductive method, proceeding from the specific to the general, the advancement of science was

greatly aided. In this way, new factors result from the fundamental processes of reasoning, whereas in the deductive method,
the emphasis is upon proving that which is known. The sciences
of biology, chemistry, and physics use the inductive method.
Another contribution was that of René Descartes (1596-1660)
who stressed the observation of facts instead of the earlier
practice of resorting to ancient authority as bases for scientific
investigations.

CHAPTER VI.

RISE OF PARLIAMENT IN ENGLAND

SIGNIFICANCE OF THE ENGLISH PARLIAMENTARY SYSTEM

England during the sixteenth and seventeenth centuries was developing the parliamentary system of government, while on the continent, especially in France, the trend was toward absolutism. The English revolutions of the seventeenth century assured the supremacy of parliament over the Crown, and established a stable, yet flexible government that has endured through two hundred and fifty years of rapidly changing history, always finding within itself the means of adaptation to new conditions. This development has had an immense influence on the general political evolution of Europe. English parliamentarianism represents one of the three main streams of historical influence that have gone into the making of modern democracy, the other two streams being the French Revolution, and the rise of laissez faire capitalism.

Early Steps Toward Parliamentary Government_ The germ of the English Parliament is to be found in the ancient Witen of the Anglo-Saxon kings, an advisory council of the chief (literally, the wise) men of the kingdom. After the Norman

43

conquest (1066) the Witen was replaced by the Great Council, composed of all who held land by feudal tenure directly from the king. It was thus originally in no sense an elective body or one representative of the English people, but it served to form a tradition that government was a joint responsibility.

MAGNA CARTA. In 1215, exasperated by the abuses of the worthless King John, a group of barons rose in rebellion and forced the king to sign the agreement called the Great Charter or *Magna Carta,* which placed restrictions on his powers. Later generations undoubtedly read into the Magna Carta a great many guarantees of civil liberty that were never in the minds of the thoroughly reactionary and self-interest seeking barons who drew it up, but in estimating its historical importance we must consider not only its original intention but its ultimate result. Reinterpreted to suit changing times, the Magna Carta was appealed to in the seventeenth century as the great bulwark of the rights of Englishmen. It served as a reminder that the subjects had once risen in arms against their monarch. It furnished a basis for self-taxation. It was the most important landmark in the tradition of the supremacy of the law as opposed to the king's arbitrary will.

BEGINNINGS OF A REPRESENTATIVE PARLIAMENT. In the middle of the thirteenth century King John's successor, Henry III, aroused great opposition by his subservience to the financial exactions of the Pope. Once more the barons resisted and obtained substantial concessions. But the most interesting result of the contest was the establishment of Parliament as an *elective* and *representative* body containing commoners as well as the great feudal lords. Early in the fourteenth century there was a formal separation of Parliament into two houses, Lords and Commons.

Progress in Fourteenth and Fifteenth Centuries. Unlike analogous representative and consultative bodies on the continent which remained rudimentary, the English Parliament continued its development through the fourteenth and fifteenth centuries and became an indispensable arm of the government. It had the sole power of taxation and its consent was necessary for legislation. Although the Tudor sovereigns in the sixteenth century established a nearly absolute monarchy, they did it by managing and overawing Parliament rather than by suppressing it. The real powers of Parliament did not die but merely slept. Even Henry VIII, the most despotic and powerful of the Tudors, did not rule by decree, as did kings and princes in continental countries.

Stuarts and the Revival of Resistance. The death of Elizabeth, the last of the Tudors, and the accession of James I in 1603 marks the beginning of a long period of friction between Parliament and the Crown. Of the many factors that contributed to this friction, three were especially conspicuous: (1) the religious controversy between the growing sect of Puritans and the conservatives who wished to maintain the Episcopal establishment and the forms and rituals that the English Church still retained from Roman Catholicism, (2) the determination of the bourgeoisie and the small landowners to resist taxation unless they could control the foreign and domestic policies of the government, and (3) the personal tactlessness and political ineptitude of the Stuart kings James I, Charles I, Charles II, and James II.

JAMES I AND PARLIAMENT. When James attempted to lay and collect taxes himself and Parliament protested, he dissolved Parliament. A further cause of annoyance to the monarch was by the Puritans, a wing of the Church of England that wished to "purify" the Church of the doctrines and rituals that were still retained from the old Catholicism. Many of them also favored a change in Church organization from the Episcopal (government of the church by a hierarchy of consecrated bishops) to the Presbyterian (government by elders selected from the congregations). This group, the Puritans, whose strength was in the middle class, were troubled by the policies of James I, and sought to combat him and his successors with the weapon of parliamentary traditions. The conciliatory policy of James with Spain and the union of Scotland with England were opposed by the merchants.

PARLIAMENT UNDER CHARLES I. The beginning of the reign of Charles I (1625), James' successor, was auspicious. He favored a war with Spain, and upon his marriage to Henrietta Maria, sister of Louis XIII of France, he promised that no concession would be granted to Roman Catholics. But Charles I had also promised Louis XIII that he would grant concessions to Catholics in England. Parliament granted Charles I money to carry on a war with Spain, but he used the money and proceeded to ask for more without showing any signs of engaging in a conflict with Spain. When the House of Commons refused further subsidies, he dissolved it. The failure of the English fleet at Cadiz, the unsuccessful attempt to help the French Huguenots at the siege of La Rochelle, and his inability to get money by forced loans so added to Charles' difficulties that he was forced to call a new parliament. In return for the grant of subsidies, Charles signed the Petition of Right (1628) promising not to levy taxes without consent of Parliament, not to quarter soldiers in private houses, not to establish martial law in times of peace, and not to order arbitrary imprisonment. Parliament asked more and more concessions and finally Charles I once more dissolved Parliament (1629) and did not call another until 1640. During this time Charles tried every possible method of getting funds. The most obnoxious way of raising revenue was the levying of "ship money" on both inland and seaboard towns. Charles also had religious troubles. He relaxed the restrictions on Catholics and reintroduced certain dogmas of the Catholic church into the Anglican. In the meantime the Puritan movement was gaining strength. Many advanced Protestants left the country and fled to America. The attempt of Charles I to interfere with the Presbyterian religion in Scotland aroused the Scotch, who swore to defend their religion. They overthrew the King's bishops and revolted. Failing to put down the rebellion, Charles I called a Parliament (1640) but dissolved it when it failed to grant the necessary funds (Short Parliament). However, he immediately had to call another to check the Scotch forces (Long Parliament, 1640-1660). By this last act Charles admitted he could not rule without the help of Parliament; divine-right monarchy had failed.

Reforms of the Long Parliament. The Long Parliament, confident that it had the upper hand, proceeded to correct certain abuses before giving Charles the necessary subsidies to check the Scotch. John Pym, John Hampden, and Oliver Cromwell were in control.

POWERS OF PARLIAMENT INCREASED. The House of Commons impeached Charles' minister, Thomas Wentworth (Earl of Strafford) and Archbishop Laud, whose arbitrary church government during the period of Charles' personal rule had aroused great resentment, and sent them to the Tower where they were later executed. Special tribunals such as the Court of Star Chamber and the High Commission were abolished. The King could no longer use irregular financial expedients, and it was finally decided that Parliament must meet at least once every three years (Triennial Act).

"CAVALIERS" AND "ROUNDHEADS." Charles never sincerely acquiesced in these reforms but schemed to get control of an army by which he might put down parliamentary opposition. In 1642 he attempted to arrest five leaders in the House of Commons but failed. The House of Commons proceeded to pass ordinances without the royal seal and issued a call to arms. Charles I called this an act of rebellion and requested his legal subjects to help put down the rebellion. The followers of the King were known as "Cavaliers," while those of the middle class supporting Parliament were called "Roundheads."

Puritan Revolution. The Great Rebellion (1642-1646) was the conflict between Cavaliers and Roundheads for control in England. The Long Parliament was predominantly Presbyterian or at least strongly Puritan; hence they formed an alliance with the Scotch, the Solemn League and Covenant (1643), agreeing to the introduction of advanced religious reform and religious uniformity in England, Ireland, and Scotland. Charles' supporters were defeated at Marston Moor (1644). When in the following year at the decisive battle of Naseby the king's cause met final ruin, the Presbyterians, after making Presbyterianism supreme, were willing to restore the king on that basis.

RUMP PARLIAMENT. The "New Model" (Ironsides) army objected to the restoration of Charles I. Under Colonel Pride, the House of Commons was rid of its Presbyterian Commoners and only the Independents remained—about sixty—to determine the policies of the nation. They composed the "Rump" Parliament which was responsible for the beheading of Charles (1649) and the establishment of a Commonwealth.

DISSOLUTION OF THE RUMP PARLIAMENT (1653). The Commonwealth proceeded to settle the troubles in England and to crush rebellion in Ireland and Scotland. Oliver Cromwell and his "New Model" army were equal to the task, and the uprisings were cruelly put down. The Rump Parliament obtained the support of the people in the Navigation Acts (1651) aimed against the Dutch, and in the indecisive trade wars with Holland, which increased English prestige. In 1653 Cromwell became disgusted with the domestic policy of the Rump and put them out.

OLIVER CROMWELL (1653-1658). By the *Instrument* of *Government* — the first written constitution — a Protectorate was established which was really a constitutional monarchy with Cromwell as Lord Protector for life. He was to govern with the aid of a small body of advisers, and Parliament was to meet at least every three years. Advanced Puritanism, either in its form of Presbyterianism or of "Independency" (practical local autonomy of church congregations), was the state religion. Cromwell, however, became a practical dictator. He owed his power to (1) support of his army, (2) the domestic prosperity which England enjoyed, and (3) his diplomacy in foreign affairs. Nevertheless, there were many sources of discontent. The failure of Cromwell's son to control the army after his father's death (1658) meant the end of the Protectorate, the restoration of the Rump Parliament and the Presbyterian members, and negotiations for the return of Charles II, who had fled to France.

Restoration of the Stuarts. Charles II (1660-1685) was restored amid great enthusiasm. The people had tired of Puritanism.

CATHOLICISM AND THE RESTORED STUARTS. The religious situation favored Charles II greatly. He readily consented to abide by Magna Carta and the Petition of Right. However, under the restored Stuarts, the history of England was one of financial and religious disputes. Both Charles II and his younger brother James had leanings toward Catholicism and absolutism. James even announced his conversion to Catholicism in 1672. Charles II attempted to get money by various means, not the least important source being the French king, Louis XIV, who gave Charles II £200,000 annually to keep out of continental affairs. In religious matters, Parliament deprived the Presbyterians of their offices (Act of Uniformity), decreed that dissenting clergymen must not come within five miles of their old churches (Five Mile Act 1665), and excluded dissenters from town offices (Corporation Act). In 1672 Charles II issued a "Declaration of Indulgence," granting religious liberty to both Roman Catholics and dissenters. This pro-Catholic act and Prince James' open acceptance of the Catholic religion caused considerable unrest. Parliament looked upon the Declaration of Indulgence as an illegal usurpation of power by the king and forced its withdrawal in 1673.

WHIGS AND TORIES. The acceptance of Catholicism by James in 1672 had stirred up Protestant Britain. Parliament was divided over the Exclusion Bill of 1679, which was an attempt to prevent James from receiving the crown because he was a Catholic. The supporters of the Exclusion Bill were called Whigs, and those opposing it, Tories. The Tories defeated the bill in the House of Lords (1680).

"Glorious Revolution." The "Glorious Revolution" definitely established the supremacy of Parliament in England.

SUPREMACY OF PARLIAMENT INSURED UNDER THE BILL OF RIGHTS (1689). James II (1685-1688) in his short reign stirred up opposition on all sides. His Declaration of Indulgence, aiming to give religious and political liberty to both Catholics and dissenters, aroused the ire of the people. The birth of a son to James II (1688) by his Catholic wife caused considerable concern, and the Whigs and Tories joined in inviting William, Prince of Orange and a grandson of Charles I, and his wife Mary, daughter of James II, to ascend the English throne (1688). James fled to France. The Bill of Rights (1689), which protected the Anglican Church and the powers of Parliament and summed up the traditional rights of English subjects under the law, was a guarantee that the king and queen would not overstep their authority. Religious toleration for dissenters was obtained by the Whigs (1689).

WHIGS IN CONTROL OF PARLIAMENT. Under William and Mary (1689-1694), and Anne (1702-1714), the Whigs were generally in control. Their foreign wars were exceedingly successful. The Union of Scotland and England (1707) was favorably accepted at this time with its common-trade regulations, customs, and excise.

HANOVERIAN KINGS. After Anne, the crown passed to the Hanoverian line, George I (1714-1727). George I took little interest in the affairs of England. He did not even trouble himself to learn the English language. In his reign the drift that had begun under Anne toward government by a group of ministers continued. This was the beginning of the modern cabinet system. The Whigs retained their power until 1761.

MINISTRIES OF ROBERT WALPOLE AND WILLIAM PITT. Under the first two Georges, Robert Walpole was the great Whig leader. He aimed to maintain peace and prosperity and to keep his majority in the House of Commons. It was he who created the concept of a leading or "prime" minister. Another great prime minister was William Pitt, Earl of Chatham, whose successful foreign policy toward Spain and France won him great popularity.

MINISTERIAL RESPONSIBILITY. Whatever the significance today of the English ministerial system, its importance in the seventeenth and eighteenth centuries was not that it was democratic, but rather that its divine-right kings could be weakened and a Parliament and group of ministers be substituted as the real rulers.

CHAPTER VII.

DEVELOPMENT OF ABSOLUTISM IN FRANCE

SEVENTEENTH CENTURY FRANCE

The rise of absolutism in France centered about the activities of Henry IV, Richelieu, and Mazarin. The settlement of foreign affairs and of the internal religious strife in a peaceful manner allowed Henry IV to turn his attention to sorely needed internal consolidation. Richelieu, the able and ambitious minister of the weak King Louis XIII, centralized the government and put down all opposition. His policies were continued by Mazarin. Upon the death of Mazarin in 1661, a smooth-working government machine came under the personal control of Louis XIV, during whose reign (1643-1715) France became the predominant power of Europe.

Henry IV (1589-1610). Henry IV had Sully, his chief minister, reform the royal finances by doing away with several abuses. In ten years he saved 10,000,000 livres. An attempt was made to promote and preserve universal peace — "Grand Design" — but it came to naught before the jealousies of ambitious sovereigns. While Sully improved the conditions of agriculture, Henry IV encouraged the middle class in its commercial pursuits.

Work of Richelieu. The work of Henry IV was partly undone during the regency of his widow, Marie de' Medici, who spent the surplus that Henry IV and Sully had accumulated and then called the Estates General (1614) to meet the situation. The internal jealousies and strife of the Estates General made it ineffectual, and Marie dismissed it. This was the last time this French representative body met until the outbreak of the great revolution in 1789. Thus while in England the power of Parliament became supreme in the government during the seventeenth century, in France the Estates General sank entirely out of sight. When Louis XIII came to power he allowed his chief minister, Richelieu, to carry on the affairs of government (1624-1642). Richelieu was determined to make the royal power supreme in France, and to make France predominant in Europe. A clear idea of the reasons for Richelieu's success in attaining these aims may be had by comparing the situation in France during this period with that of England. There were three main differences: (1) the ruthless energy and political skill of Richelieu himself as compared with the incompetence of the Stuart kings and their advisers in England, (2) the fact that in France taxation was imposed only on the leaderless and unorganized Third Estate or Commons, so that no strong coalition of nobles, clergy, and commoners could be formed to resist tax levies, and (3) the fact that the Calvinist Protestants (Huguenots) in France were weaker than the corresponding Puritan group in England.

LACK OF A REPRESENTATIVE ASSEMBLY. Richelieu first of all encouraged the king to carry on his business by personal appointees and not by a representative assembly. The Royal Council became the supreme lawmaking and administrative body.

ARMY IMPROVED. The Royal Army was increased and made responsible to the Crown. France was to have the best army in Europe.

TREATMENT OF THE HUGUENOTS. Absolutism was furthered by taking from the Huguenots certain political privileges which made them dangerous to the monarchy. The Huguenots resisted but were put down after much bloodshed. Their final stand was made at La Rochelle, which capitulated only after a desperate siege lasting more than a year (1627-1628). They were allowed to worship in freedom and to hold political offices, but they had to give up their fortifications and assemblies (Edict of Alais, 1629).

NOBLES WEAKENED. Richelieu also bolstered up absolutism by weakening the nobles. He introduced an espionage system, destroyed fortifications which were not needed for foreign defense, and mercilessly crushed attempts at rebellion.

INTENDANTS REPLACED GOVERNORS. French administration was also centralized by appointing intendants responsible to the crown in place of the old noble governors. These intendants were given much power, but the king could remove any or all at his pleasure.

RICHELIEU'S FOREIGN POLICY. The Thirty Years' War (1618-1648) gave Richelieu the opportunity to interfere effectively in general European affairs. Although a Roman Catholic cardinal, Richelieu was above all concerned with the aggrandizement of the power of France. He cared little for the religious issues involved. The effect of his intervention was to prevent a clear-cut victory in the struggle of the Imperialist forces of the Hapsburgs, and to prolong the war until the possible rivals of France (Spain and the Empire) were thoroughly exhausted and unable to prevent France from assuming a dominant position. Richelieu died in 1642, six years before the final liquidation of the war in the Peace of Westphalia, but he had the satisfaction of seeing his main policies on the road to success.

Cardinal Mazarin. During the minority of Louis XIV, Cardinal Mazarin, an Italian who became a naturalized Frenchman, succeeded Richelieu and governed France until his death in 1661. Cardinal Mazarin continued Richelieu's policies and further strengthened absolutism under Louis XIV, in spite of the opposition of the Fronde.

ACTIVITIES OF THE FRONDE (1648-1652). The Fronde was a popular protest against Mazarin's interference with the Parlement of Paris (judicial body). The Parlement's duty was to register the laws and edicts of the king. When the Parlement of Paris defied Mazarin and refused to register a law and called other laws and acts illegal, Mazarin had to recognize its power until the army returned from Germany; but on its return he easily put down the trouble and instituted the old laws again. Several uprisings followed, but they were not of much consequence.

SIGNIFICANCE OF THE FRONDE. As a result of the Fronde (1) the nobles were discredited more, (2) the Parlement was. forbidden to devote attention to political or financial affairs, (3) Paris was disarmed, and (4) the royal power was more absolute than ever.

THIRTY YEARS' WAR

The Thirty Years' War was a series of conflicts (1618-1648) in which most of the powers of Europe became involved. In its origin it was a religious struggle between the new Protestant religion and the Roman Catholic Counter-Reformation. The religious issues soon became obscured by personal and political issues, however. Its great importance in European history arises from its three main results: (1) it proved that neither Catholicism nor Protestantism could destroy the other and thus forced a *modus vivendi* upon hitherto implacably hostile religious groups; (2) it ruined for more than a century the economic and political power of the German-speaking peoples, gave the finishing stroke to the movement toward German national unity that had seemed a live possibility in the early days of the Lutheran movement, and thus elevated France to the dominant position in continental Europe; (3) it was the most important landmark in the rise of the European national State system.

Causes of the Thirty Years' War. The fundamental cause of the Thirty Years' War was the explosive religious, economic, and social discontent that had been building up in the German countries ever since the Lutheran revolt. But what began as a civil war within the Holy Roman Empire immediately became international in scope, as outside powers strove to take advantage of the situation to promote their dynastic interests or to further the cause of their co-religionists.

RELIGIOUS UNREST. The religious Peace of Augsburg (1555) was unsatisfactory to many elements. It did not establish a principle of toleration (the very idea of toleration was practically unheard-of in the sixteenth century) but attempted in the famous *cuius regio, eius religio* clause to impose in each separate state (of which there were about 300) the religion of the reigning prince. This provision led to endless friction. No generally accepted agreement had been reached regarding the disposition of church lands when a state or individual churchman became Protestant. The Emperor Charles V, by imperial decree, prohibited any further secularization of Catholic Church lands, but the decree was generally disregarded. The Augsburg settlement left the Reformed or Calvinist religion entirely outside the pale, and during the latter half of the sixteenth century there was a considerable increase in the number of Calvinists in the Empire, particularly in Bohemia.

POLITICAL STRUGGLES. A second important factor in the explosive condition of the Germanies at the opening of the seventeenth century was the political rivalry between the princes, who wished to secure for themselves a greater degree of sovereignty and independence, and the emperor, who desired to establish a strong central monarchy. It has been apparent in the cases of England, France, and Spain how this struggle between feudal decentralization and strong monarchial government is one of the leading characteristics of the transition from medieval to modern times. In the Germanies, because of the greater power of the princes, the struggle was much more prolonged and intense, and in the end it resulted not in the establishment of a strong national monarchy, but in a hopeless disunity and disintegration.

SOCIAL AND ECONOMIC DISCONTENT. To the religious and political factors making for trouble must be added the widespread discontent of the lower classes throughout the Empire. All the terrible conditions that had produced the desperate Peasants' Revolt of 1525 remained unreformed, and it was easy for a leader to collect a private army of men who had nothing to lose and who felt no loyalty except to the prospect of plunder.

DYNASTIC RIVALRIES IN THE THIRTY YEARS' WAR. In its later phases (1630-1648) the Thirty Years' War became predominately a struggle between the Hapsburgs on the one hand and the kings of Sweden and Cardinal Richelieu of France on the other. From this point of view, the war was a chapter in the long French-

German rivalry that began with the wars of Francis I and
Charles V and has continued with more or less lengthy inter-
ruptions throughout modern history.

Periods of Thirty Years' War. The four phases of the
Thirty Years' War were (1) Bohemian Revolt, (2) Danish Period,
(3) Swedish Period, and (4) French Period.

BOHEMIAN REVOLT (1618). The Bohemian Revolt aimed
to prevent the Catholic, Ferdinand II, from receiving the crown
of the Holy Roman Empire upon the death of Matthias (1612-
1619) for fear that some of the religious freedom would be lost.
The Bohemians broke in upon a meeting of Ferdinand's envoys,
pitched them out of the window, and proceeded to declare Ferdinand deposed as king of Bohemia, and to crown in his stead
the Protestant, Frederick, Elector of the Palatinate. However,
Ferdinand's forces drove out Frederick, the Bohemian nobles were
punished, the Protestant religion was forbidden, and Frederick's
lands were confiscated.

DANISH PERIOD (1625-1629). The Danish intervention was
brought on by Christian IV, who was opposed to Hapsburg control of his Holstein dukedom, who wanted to extend his sway
over the North Sea ports, and to champion Lutheranism. With
the aid of English money and the troops of Calvinist and Lutheran
princes of Germany, Christian IV invaded Germany, but the combined forces of Count Tilly and the mercenary army of Wallenstein were too much for him. He consented to the Peace of
Lübeck (1629), which made him give up many German bishoprics,
although he was allowed to keep Jutland, Schleswig, and Holstein.
As a result of these successes, the Catholic League of German
Princes persuaded Ferdinand to issue an Edict of Restitution
(1629), which restored to the Church all property which had
been confiscated in violation of the Peace of Augsburg.

SWEDISH PERIOD (1630-1635). The Swedish Period was
caused by the ambition of Gustavus Adolphus to make Sweden
the leading Protestant state in northern Europe. The Edict of
Restitution created ill feeling in the Germanies, and with the
promise of aid from France, Gustavus thought the time was ripe
to gain territory in northern Germany. At first Gustavus was

successful and gained the support of powerful Protestant princes. In desperation the Emperor, Ferdinand II, recalled Wallenstein, who had been exiled due to agitation by the Catholics and gave him full power to check the Swedes. In the Battle of Lützen (1632) Gustavus was killed. Wallenstein was later assassinated by an imperialist who feared that he was conspiring against the Emperor. Without a leader, the Swedes were ready for peace. The Treaty of Prague (1635) closed the Swedish Period of the war in a manner less satisfactory from the Hapsburg standpoint than either the Bohemian or Danish revolts. The Edict of Restitution was practically withdrawn, and the Church lands were to be left for forty years in the hands of the holders as of November 12, 1627.

FRENCH PERIOD (1635-1648). The foreign policy of Richelieu to make France supreme in Europe wrecked the Treaty of Prague. He was not only eager to curb the Austrian Hapsburgs but also desirous of humbling Spain, whose possessions surrounded him. At first the French suffered serious set-backs, but Richelieu kept sending fresh armies into Spanish territories. He stirred up the Portuguese against Spain, and they recovered their freedom. Mazarin continued the war after the death of Richelieu with new and brilliant leaders, the Prince of Condé and Turenne. French victories quickly followed. The Peace of Westphalia (1648), which brought the war to an end provided that (1) the German states were declared to be independent sovereignties; (2) France received Alsace (except the city of Strassburg); Metz, Toul, and Verdun were recognized as French bishoprics; (3) Sweden obtained territory in Pomerania and the Bishopric of Bremen; (4) France and Sweden received votes in the Diet of the Holy Roman Empire; (5) Brandenburg obtained eastern Pomerania and several bishoprics; (6) the Rhenish Palatinate was divided between Maximilian of Bavaria and the son of the deposed Frederick; (7) Switzerland and Holland were recognized as independent; (8) Calvinists were to share all the privileges of the Lutherans; (9) all church property was to be held by those who held it in January, 1624; and (10) an equal number of Protestant and Catholic judges were to sit in the imperial courts.

Conditions in the Holy Roman Empire (1648). The Peace of Westphalia still further weakened the Holy Roman Empire. The economic conditions after the war were unbearable. Villages and cities had been destroyed, the population dwindled, industries were at a standstill, and the morals of the people declined.

HUMILIATION OF SPAIN (1659). The French continued the conflict against Spain, and with the military leadership of Turenne the Spanish were completely routed. The Treaty of the Pyrenees (1659) further increased the power of France and the prestige of the French king, Louis XIV.

INTERNATIONAL LAW. The beginnings of international law are found in this period. The appearance of a real state-system in Europe, based on the equality and sovereignty of the independent states, dates from this period. Permanent embassies were established in foreign countries, and international customs grew up. Hugo Grotius published his work *On the Law of War and Peace* (1625) and turned men to the idea of international laws to protect neutral nations and to prevent wanton destruction of life and property.

┌─────────────────────────────┐

Significant **Dates**

Reign of Louis XIV . . 1643-1715

Edict of Nantes Revoked . . 1685

Peace of Utrecht 1713

Death of Louis XIV . . . 1715

└─────────────────────────────┘

CHAPTER VIII.

AGE OF LOUIS XIV, 1661-1715

GRAND MONARCH

The work of Mazarin and his predecessors made possible the absolutism of Louis XIV. Absolutism, according to Bossuet, (a) made the person of the king sacred, (b) made him a paternal guardian of the people's welfare, (c) made him accountable to God alone for his acts, and (d) caused him to be selected by divine right to rule. Louis XIV was the supreme example of absolutism. Known throughout Europe as the Grand Monarch, he was the model that lesser princes strove to imitate, at once the embodiment and the justification of the theory of government that was to prevail in Europe down to the time of the French Revolution.

Court of Louis XIV. Louis XIV surrounded himself with capable advisers and lieutenants. At Versailles he was served by nobles who, without political power, revelled in a social life at the King's palace. Leaders in the arts patronized by Louis XIV, they came to Versailles to display their talents. Under Louis' patronage Versailles became the intellectual and cultural capital of Europe as well as the center of fashion and social life. Some of the greatest figures of French literature flourished during this period: the dramatists, Corneille (1606-1684), Molière (1622-

1673), and Racine (1639-1699) ; the poets, La Fontaine (1621-1695), and Boileau-Despréaux (1636-1711) ; and the keen observers of human nature, La Rochefoucald (1613-1680), La Bruyère (1645-1696), and Madame de Sévigné (1626-1696).

Colbert, the Financial Minister. Jean Baptiste Colbert (1619-1683) was one of Louis' most important advisers. His greatest work was in the financial field, where he introduced the budget system. He attempted to ease the tax burden of the peasants by correcting the abuses of tax-collecting and by instituting a system of indirect taxation. Colbert also fostered mercantilism, the theory of national economy that held that commerce should be regulated so as to secure a "favorable balance of trade" which should result in building up the stocks of precious metals within the country. To protect his new commerce Colbert fitted out a royal navy that was not insignificant when compared to that of England, Holland, or Spain. He also encouraged a strong colonial policy which bore fruit in French possessions in Canada, Louisiana, the West Indies, India, and Madagascar.

Louvois and the French Army. Lacking in personal military ability, Louis XIV surrounded himself with the best military brains in the land. François Michel Louvois (1641-1691) developed the French army until it was without a peer in Europe at that time. He introduced stern regulations, a distinctive military uniform, the practice of marching in step, and promotions dependent upon merit rather than social position. Vauban, the engineer, built great military fortifications for him, and Condé and Turenne were able generals. This great military machine was an excessive financial burden.

Revocation of the Edict of Nantes (1685). One of the greatest mistakes of Louis XIV was his Revocation of the Edict of Nantes (1685), and his reintroduction of religious persecution through the "dragonnades." As a result, thousands of the Huguenots migrated to Protestant countries and became useful citizens among France's enemies. The Huguenot emigration was particularly disastrous economically, because the Huguenots were, in general, the most enterprising and industrious class in France.

LOUIS XIV'S FOREIGN WARS

Louis XIV continued the work of Richelieu and Mazarin in humbling the Hapsburgs of Spain and Austria. He set out to secure natural boundaries for France — the Pyrenees, the Alps, the Rhine, and the Atlantic Ocean. His reign was rife with foreign wars for this purpose.

War of Devolution (1667-1668). His first conflict, the "War of Devolution," was an attempt of Louis XIV to wrest the Spanish Netherlands from his weak brother-in-law, Charles II of Spain. He would have quickly overcome the Netherlands had not the trade war between England and Holland come to an abrupt end. These two countries plus Sweden formed a triple alliance and had the "balance of power." Louis XIV dared not continue, so he negotiated the treaty of Aix-la-Chapelle (1668), which gave France a section of Flanders but left Spain most of the Spanish Netherlands.

Dutch War (1672-1678). Louis' second war, that with the Dutch, was brought on because of Holland's increased commercial importance and because Louis felt that Holland was responsible for the formation of the Triple Alliance that had thwarted him in the War of Devolution. Louis successfully broke up the Triple Alliance by giving the English king (Charles II) a large sum of money and by using money to prevent Sweden from supporting Holland. Having thus isolated his enemy, Louis declared war in 1672, easily occupied Lorraine, and started for Amsterdam. The Dutch, however, put William of Orange in charge, and he cut the dikes and stopped the advance of the French. The refusal of France to accept Holland's generous terms for peace made the Emperor Leopold and the Great Elector of Brandenburg join with Holland. Later Spain and several German states came in, but Turenne kept on winning French victories. Not until the English joined the allies of Holland did Louis XIV make peace. The Treaty of Nijmwegen (1678) made Spain give up the Franche Comté and several strong fortresses in the Belgian Netherlands. Holland did not lose any territory. France had proceeded a step nearer the Rhine, but the French treasury was empty, the border provinces were devastated, Turenne had been killed, and Condé had resigned. A significant feature of the Dutch War was the evidence it gave that nearly all Europe was now ready to combine to prevent further French aggrandizement. From this time forth Louis faced more determined and powerful coalitions.

War of the League of Augsburg (War of the Palatinate) (1688-1697). The War of the League of Augsburg (cf. page 66) resulted from Louis' attempts to extend further the French boundaries by claiming territories based on old feudal ties. The Emperor Leopold formed the League of Augsburg made up of Spain, Sweden, and several German princes interested in preserving the Holy Roman Empire. Louis XIV counted on England's remaining neutral, but the "Glorious Revolution" (1688) brought to the English throne the arch enemy of Louis XIV, William of Orange. William joined the League of Augsburg and declared war on France. Although France was able to win several land battles, she failed on the sea and finally in 1697 Louis sued for peace. The Treaty of Ryswick (1697) did not take away any of Louis' new possessions except the towns granted him by the Chambers of Reunion, but he was greatly humiliated. The Dutch were allowed to garrison the chief fortresses of the Spanish Netherlands, and a favorable commercial treaty was granted to them. Louis XIV had to recognize William III as king of England, restore Lorraine to its duke, and give up his claim to the Palatinate.

WAR OF SPANISH SUCCESSION

The War of Spanish Succession (1702-1713) offered Louis a final hope for making France supreme in Europe (cf. page 66). Charles II of Spain was without a male heir, so Louis dared to hope that the succession would fall to his wife, the eldest sister of Charles II, in spite of the Treaty of Pyrenees (1659) in which he renounced all claim to the Spanish throne. If the Emperor Leopold obtained the Spanish territory, it would mean a vast empire controlled by the Hapsburgs; if Louis XIV gained the inheritance, it would mean a great Bourbon empire would be created and the European "balance of power" destroyed. Although the whole of Europe was concerned about the settlement, England was especially interested as she hoped to continue to hold the balance of power.

Course of the War. Charles II made a will in which the grandson of Louis XIV, Philip of Anjou, was to be his successor. Immediately the Grand Alliance was formed with England, Holland, Austria, and several German Electors, joined later by Portugal and Savoy. The Allies demanded that the Spanish crown go to the Archduke Charles, grandson of the Emperor Leopold. The great struggle in Europe took place in the Netherlands, the southern Germanies, Italy and Spain. At first the superior resources of the allies and the brilliant generalship of the English leader the Duke of Marlborough and the leader of the Austrian armies, Prince Eugene of Savoy, won battle after battle from the French, notably Blenheim (1704), Ramillies (1706), Oudenarde (1708), and Malplaquet (1709). However, circumstances changed, Louis XIV aroused the patriotism of this people, a change of ministry in England cooled the ardor of that country for war, and the ascension of the Archduke Charles to the Austrian crown made him an undesirable candidate for the Spanish throne. Under these conditions the treaties of Utrecht, Rastadt, and Baden were signed (1713-1714).

Significance of the Peace of Utrecht-Rastadt. The Peace of Utrecht-Rastadt brought to an end the rivalry between the Bourbons of France and the Hapsburgs of Spain. However, eighteenth century France was to direct its dynastic policies against the Austrian Hapsburgs. The treaty also marked the emergence of England as' an important power in continental affairs. The period of French ascendance in Europe was ended. The appearance on the European stage of Prussia and Savoy foreshadowed a time when these would become the basis for the unification of Italy and Germany.

CHAPTER IX.

COLONIAL RIVALRY BETWEEN FRANCE AND GREAT BRITAIN

COLONIAL STRUGGLE

Throughout the seventeenth century the colonization movement was going steadily forward. But Spain and Portugal, which had acquired a commanding lead in the sixteenth century, now gave way to England and France. A part of the Portuguese empire in the east fell into the hands of the Dutch, and Spain, as a consequence of poor internal organization, unambitious leadership and foreign wars, lost her rank as a great power. The English and the French now became the great colonizing nations and world rivals. From 1689 to 1763 the struggle went on as a kind of chorus to the drama being played in Europe. Each of the great European wars had its counterpart in America and (later) in India. This colonial struggle was of immense consequence for later European and world history. We have only to think of the position of the British Empire in the contemporary world to realize what great issues hung on these apparently obscure wars far removed from the center of European interest.

Stage for the English Colonies. The English colonial movement spread to North America, to Africa, and to India.

64

NORTH AMERICA. The English claim to North America rested on the voyage of John Cabot (1497). English settlements which had been made at Newfoundland, around Hudson Bay, and from Maine to South Carolina, grew in population and wealth, until in 1688 there were over 300,000 Englishmen in America. They had transplanted English civilization to the New World and were busily engaged in pushing back the frontier, exploring and settling new regions, fighting the Indians and building up an important commerce in negro slaves, tobacco, and other merchandise.

AFRICA. At this time, the basis for Britain's claims to Africa were laid. The English established trading posts in Africa where they might obtain gold-dust, ivory and negro slaves, but colonization there was delayed until the nineteenth century.

INDIA. In India the English were intent upon establishing trading centers, not upon colonization. The loose government of the Mohammedan Moguls made it possible for European countries to step in and set up trading posts. The English by 1688 were established at (a) Calcutta, (b) Madras, and (c) Bombay. This commercial penetration of India did not imply political control by the English government; the agency of penetration was the privately owned East India Company, chartered in 1600.

Theatre of French Colonization. France also sought colonies and trading posts in America, Africa, and India.

NORTH AMERICA. In North America the French settled along the St. Lawrence and laid claim to the basin of the Mississippi. French forts were built along the "Great River." Since English and French claims overlapped, it was inevitable that these countries would clash sooner or later.

AFRICA. Beginnings were also made in Africa with settlements along the Senegal River, at Gorée and in Madagascar. These trading posts served as a basis for French commerce in Africa and as tangible evidence of attempted colonization.

INDIA. In India the French competed with the English for trade. The French posts at Chandarnaga and Pondicherry were too near Calcutta and Madras respectively, not to arouse suspicion and jealousy.

Basis of Colonial Supremacy. The contest for colonial supremacy was to be decided not by the validity of prior settlement but rather by the fighting power of the two countries.

ENGLISH NAVY AN ELEMENT OF STRENGTH. The English were stronger than the French from a naval standpoint. Since the defeat of the Spanish Armada (1588), England's navy was becoming stronger and stronger. The navy also had been able to keep back the Dutch in the commercial wars with that country.

COLONIAL POLICIES OF FRANCE AND ENGLAND. The French colonial policy had certain aspects which were worthy of note. New France (Canada) was recognized as a royal province, and the French were on better terms with the natives than were the English. In terms of larger numbers of Europeans in her colonies, England had a decided advantage. Whereas the Huguenots had been refused a haven in New France, the English opened their colonies to religious exiles.

COLONIAL WARS

King William's War (1689-1697). King William's War (1689-1697) in America corresponded to the War of the League of Augsburg (cf. page 62). King William's War was entirely indecisive. It is interesting, however, to note that the French were successful in enlisting the Indians on their side, a feature that continued throughout the English-French struggle in North America. The Peace of Ryswick (1697) restored the situation in America to the status quo preceding the war.

Queen Anne's War (1702-1713). Queen Anne's War (1702-1713) was the American phase of the War of the Spanish Succession (cf. page 62). The French once more sent Indians to burn the English settlements in New England and the English attacked Port Royal and Quebec. Port Royal was captured in 1710. The attempt to capture Quebec and Montreal failed. However, the English navy managed to humble the French fleet and drive her privateers from the sea. The Treaty of Utrecht (1713) brought this war to an end. France ceded Newfoundland, Nova Scotia, and Hudson Bay to England.

NORTH AMERICA
·1763·

Scale of Miles
0 100 200 300 400 500   1000

French Fortifications in America and India. After Utrecht France began to strengthen her position in America and India. Fortresses were erected on the St. Lawrence, the Great Lakes, and the Mississippi to protect French interests. In India, the rise of French influence is notable as a result of the work of the governor-general, Dupleix, who was appointed in 1741. Not the least of his accomplishments was the enlisting and training of native troops ("Sepoys"). Dupleix fortified his capital, Pondicherry.

King George's War (1744-1748). The third conflict, King George's War (1744-1748), opened as a result of trouble with Spain over the Asiento (1713). Both the English and Spanish had grievances to report. The "War of Jenkin's Ear" between England and Spain (1739) was a prelude to renewed fighting between England and France. The war in Europe was the War of the Austrian Succession (1740-1748 cf. page 81). In King George's War, the English colonists under Colonel William Pepperell, captured Louisburg (1745) but by the Treaty of Aix-la-Chapelle, it was returned to the French. In India the French succeeded in taking Madras, but the English fleet was about to capture Dupleix at Pondicherry when peace was signed in Europe. Madras was returned to the English, and the privileges of the Asiento (the slave trade concession in the Spanish West Indies) were revoked by Spain, Great Britain receiving a money settlement.

SEVEN YEARS' WAR

The Seven Years' War (1756-1763) in Europe and India (cf. page 82) and the French and Indian War (1754-1763) in North America definitely made England supreme in America and France's ambition for a great colonial empire a lost desire. France was defeated in Europe by the armies of Frederick the Great of Prussia; her naval power was all but completely ruined by the British; in India the Frenchman Dupleix was forced to admit defeat before the Englishman Clive; and in America, New France (Canada) became a British province.

French and Indian War (1754-1763). The French and Indian War was opened first as a contest for the Ohio Valley.

The French continued to build forts, and the English finally started construction of one at the junction of the Monongahela and Allegheny rivers—a strategic position. The French, however, seized the new fort, named it Duquesne and were able to hold it against a small force under George Washington. With Fort Niagara and Fort Duquesne lost, the English built two new forts —Fort Edward and Fort William Henry on Lake George. When William Pitt became Prime Minister in England (1757), he stirred up the country and raised a new army of colonial volunteers. In two years they had succeeded in capturing the French strongholds of Louisburg (1758), Fort Duquesne (1758), Fort Ticonderoga (1759), and Fort Niagara (1759). By great strategy, the English leader, Wolfe, with a few thousand followers scaled the cliff and reached the Plains of Abraham outside Quebec. Montcalm, the French leader, quickly drew up his troops for a battle, which the English won and Quebec surrendered. Both Wolfe and Montcalm lost their lives in this battle (1759). The next year Montreal fell and New France was England's.

Seven Years' War in India. In India also, France was destined to suffer defeat at the hands of the English. Dupleix's attempts to gain political power in India were prevented by Robert Clive, a young Englishman. He successfully prevented Dupleix from controlling Carnatic by taking Arcot (1751). Clive also revenged the "Black Hole" episode, making the nawab (ruler) give up Calcutta. He captured the French post of Chandarnagar. The victory at Plassey (1757), the capture of Masulipatan, and the fall of Pondicherry (1761) made England supreme in India. Officially, these exploits of Clive were undertaken on behalf of the East India Company, but the Company had now become almost an arm of the government. In 1773 definite legislation was adopted making the Company partially responsible to the Crown, and vesting in the Company's agents judicial and other governmental powers.

Treaty of Paris (1763). The Treaty of Paris (1763) left France only two small islands off the coast of Newfoundland (St. Pierre and Miquelon), a few islands in the West Indies, and a foothold in Guiana in South America. Great Britain received from France the· St. Lawrence valley as a result of the treaty. The French were allowed to have trading posts in India but were not permitted to maintain troops or build forts.

Significance of Treaty of Paris. The Treaty of Paris, which had to do with colonial expansion, is one of the most important treaties because it definitely made Great Britain the greatest colonizing country, and the greatest maritime power. It ruined, temporarily at least, the colonial and commercial ambitions of France.

CHAPTER X.

BRITISH COLONIAL EMPIRE

MERCANTILIST THEORY

The Mercantilist believed that Colonies existed (a) to furnish the mother country with goods which could not be produced at home, (b) to trade with the mother country alone and not compete with her industries or enrich her commercial rivals, (c) to help bear the burden of the home government, and (d) to enable the mother country to build up a "favorable balance of trade," i.e. a flow of precious metals into the country. This system was put into practice with the American colonies.

Colonial Production. Commodities which England could not produce were encouraged in the colonies. Governmental favors were showered on these goods so that England would not have to be dependent upon other countries for them.

Protection of Industries of Mother Country. Industries at home (England) were protected by prohibiting the colonies from manufacturing and exporting such goods as were in direct competition with English products. The hat manufacturers in America, for example, could not manufacture for export. Woolen fabrics could not be exported, and the colonists were not allowed to manufacture wrought iron. At first these regulations were poorly enforced, and the colonists did not seriously object.

Colonial Commerce Controlled by England. Attempts to prevent England's rivals from having any commerce with the colonies became a principal cause of contention. The Navigation Acts (1651-1750) provided that (a) all export and import trade must be carried in ships built in England, Ireland or the colonies and manned by British subjects, (b) certain goods like sugar, tobacco, cotton, indigo, rice, and furs could be exported only to English ports, and (c) all goods imported into the colonies must go by way of England and pay duties there. These restrictions were tolerated only because (a) they were poorly enforced, (b) the colonists needed the help of England against the French, and (c) they did not have the means of resisting England. Before the French and Indian War they were not united in industry, social conditions, or in religion. Each colony was largely independent of its neighbor.

Attitude of Colonists Toward England in 1763. After the French and Indian War the colonists were rid of the French, and their experience in fighting gave them self-confidence. As the British government became more oppressive, the colonists became more independent. The same English tradition of opposition to absolutism which had been instrumental in bringing about Magna Carta, Petition of Right, and the Bill of Rights served now as an incentive for the American colonists. Over one hundred years of experience in practical self-government made it more difficult for an ambitious king to bring the colonists under strict control. However, the new king, George III, was desirous of gaining power. He sought to control Parliament through the appointment of George Grenville as Prime Minister (1763-1765). Grenville was favorable to the King's colonial policy a part of which was to make the colonists help pay for the British soldiers stationed in America to protect the colonists from the French and Indians. The Sugar Act (1764) and the Stamp Act (1765) were passed as a means of collecting the colonists' share of the expenses. The Navigation Acts were revived and enforced.

Right of Taxation. The colonies stoutly denied England's right to tax them without representation, but England replied that they did have representation in Parliament. They reiterated that only their own assemblies could tax them. A Stamp Act Congress (1765) was held which formally protested the Stamp Act and issued a declaration of rights. Popular disapproval was shown everywhere, and Parliament finally repealed the Act but claimed the right to tax the colonists.

PARLIAMENT AND THE COLONIES

The dispute continued to be agitated through the years 1765-1775. On the one hand the mother country was insistent that the power of taxation be recognized, while on the other, the colonies were just as determined that England should not tax them, even if it came to a question of fighting.

Colonial Reaction to the Townshend Acts (1767). The Townshend Acts (1767) levied a duty on glass, lead, painter's colors, papers, and tea—the duty to be collected in America. Infractions of the law were to be tried in court without juries. The people immediately protested, and British imports declined. Troops were sent to America to intimidate Boston, but as a result of the annoying tactics of the people, finally the soldiers fired upon them and killed four—Boston Massacre (1770).

Boston Tea Party (1773). A new Prime Minister, Lord North (1770), repealed all the Townshend duties except the three pence tax on tea. The colonists, however, refused to yield to the principles of Parliamentary taxation and retaliated by emptying the tea from a British ship into Boston Harbor (Boston Tea Party, 1773).

Intolerable Acts (1774). The reply to the Boston Tea Party from England was the Five Intolerable Acts (1774), which (a) closed Boston Harbor, (b) deprived Massachusetts of self-government, (c) provided for the trial in England of royal officers who committed offenses in the colonies, (d) allowed royal troops to be quartered in the home, and (e) extended the province of Quebec to the Ohio and recognized The Roman Catholic Church in that province.

AMERICAN REVOLUTION

The time for conciliation passed and the American War for Independence became a fact. Previous to 1774 the American colonists had had no choice but to put up with the burdens imposed by the mother country. After this date the French no longer represented a real menace to their development. Further, the union of the colonies for military purposes served as an example of union for political means.

Significance of Events of 1775. The Battle of Lexington (April 19, 1775), the First and Second Continental Congresses (1774-1775), and the Declaration of Independence (July, 1776), definitely severed the colonies from the mother country. At first England did not realize the seriousness of the revolt; when she did, it was too late.

European Allies of Colonies. The victory of the colonies at Saratoga (1777) not only gave the colonists courage but resulted in the war's assuming a European character. Recognizing the possibility of American success after Saratoga, France openly joined the Colonists (1778). Spain and Holland joined with France and the colonists to humiliate Great Britain. Most of the rest of Europe adhered to the Armed Neutrality of Russia, and Great Britain was without allies.

War in Europe. The war in Europe found Spain, Holland, and France attacking the British Empire at all points. For the most part they were unsuccessful, succeeding in obtaining only the island of Minorca in the Mediterranean.

Surrender at Yorktown (1781). In North America, the colonists with the aid of the French on land and sea were able to defeat the English leader, Cornwallis, at Yorktown (1781), and compel him to surrender. Harassed by France, Spain, and Holland, England deemed it unwise to send additional men and supplies to America.

French Successes in India. In India the English were successful at first, but the victories of the French Admiral Suffren gave the French control of the Bay of Bengal.

Treaties of Paris and Versailles (1783). England was ready for peace and the treaties of Paris and Versailles (1783) were drawn up.

TREATY OF PARIS. By the Treaty of Paris the thirteen colonies were recognized as the independent United States of America with fishing rights on the Newfoundland banks and the right of navigation on the Mississippi. Other treaties were signed in 1795 by the newly created Republic to settle additional questions. The Jay Treaty was with England and the Pinckney Treaty with Spain.

TREATY OF VERSAILLES. By the Treaty of Versailles, France was given Tobago of the West Indies and she regained Bengal in India. Spain received the Island of Minorca and the territory of Florida. Holland arranged a separate treaty with Great Britain the following year.

A NEW COLONIAL POLICY

The lesson of the American War was not lost on the English. They began a policy of conciliation and administrative reform. The creation and development of a self-governing republic influenced the new-colonial attitude of England. The French in Canada were allowed to keep their Catholic religion (1774) and the Canadians were later given a representative assembly (1791). In India, a Board of Control was established (1784) which acted as a check on the East India Company. Finally, Ireland was given the right to make her own local laws (1782-1801).

Failure of Mercantilism. The influence of her experience in America and Adam Smith's *Wealth of Nations* led England to change her commercial policy and gradually cast off mercantilism. The fallacy of the strict observance of the theory of mercantilism became evident since the only means available for offsetting an unfavorable balance of trade was through commerce with sources other than the mother country.

Consolidation of Empire. Great Britain proceeded to weld her old world possessions to the Empire. The wars of Clive in India were supplemented by the work of Hastings (1775-1785) and Cornwallis.

REFORMS OF HASTINGS IN INDIA. Warren Hastings worked tirelessly trying to improve the India situation. He advocated having the British headquarters at Calcutta, and a thorough reform of police, military, and financial systems.

CORNWALLIS IN INDIA. Cornwallis succeeded Hastings and was successful in organizing the tax system and in extending the English control over India. After the British government took over India from the East India Company (1858), it had a vast empire which stretched from the Himalayas to the Indian Ocean and from the Indus River to the Brahmaputra.

NEW POSSESSIONS. About this time England also gained control of the Straits Settlement thereby gaining control of the Malay Peninsula and of Australia, which was valuable as a future home for English speaking people. Today the island continent has a population of nearly seven million people and an area over three times as great as that of the Thirteen Colonies.

CHAPTER XI.

THE GERMANIES

POLITICAL, SOCIAL, AND ECONOMIC CONDITIONS

Political Organization. The Holy Roman Empire still existed formally and tended slightly to hold the Germanies together politically. The Emperor at the head, a Diet composed of representatives of the princes, and a group of electors made up the frame-work, but the whole system was on the decline. The Hapsburg Emperors, as the monarchs of their hereditary Austrian territories, were powerful princes, but they exercised little leadership in the non-Austrian Germanies.

Social and Economic Situation. The outlook was very unsatisfactory. Half the population and two thirds of the movable property had been lost during the Thirty Years' War. Schools and churches were closed. The German peasants were worse off than those of any other country in Europe. Economic conditions were almost unbelievable. Economic expansion and colonial enterprise were left to other countries. A strong middle class was lacking.

Petty Sovereigns. The German princes, however, with no interference from the Emperor, the Diet, or the church, proceeded to profit from the situation. They continued to confiscate church property and to get rid of local assemblies. They travelled to France and came home to set up miniature courts like that of Louis XIV at Versailles, becoming the objects of much humor.

HEREDITARY HAPSBURG DOMINIONS

Lands of Charles VI (Holy Roman Emperor, 1711-1740). Charles VI had the following hereditary possessions: Austria proper on the Danube, Inner Austria (Styria, Corinthea and Carniola), Further Austria (Tyrol), and Upper Austria (Breisgau on the upper Rhine), Bohemia, Silesia, Moravia, and parts of Hungary with Croatia, Slavonia, and Transylvania. To these dominions Charles VI added by conquest the non-German peoples of the Belgian Netherlands, Milan, and the Kingdom of the two Sicilies. The effective control of these lands challenged the emperors and forced them to extend themselves to meet the domestic and foreign problems during the eighteenth century.

Disunity in the Hapsburg Dominions. The lack of unity in the Hapsburg dominions was a source of great weakness.

HETEROGENEOUS POPULATION. The only real bond of union was the Hapsburg Emperor. The people spoke many different languages, their customs were different, and their interests were divergent.

DOMESTIC AND FOREIGN ANIMOSITY. The Hapsburgs were unable to weld the Germanies into a powerful state because of the jealousies of the German princes and of the intervention of foreign powers (Sweden and France). However, the Hapsburgs still retained power through their prestige.

Charles VI and His Heir. Charles VI, like the Spanish Hapsburgs, did not have a male heir who could step into his place, so he set about to settle the inheritance before his death.

PRAGMATIC SANCTION. Early in his reign he promulgated a Pragmatic Sanction, which said that his dominions were indivisible and that they could be inherited by female heirs in default of male. By this Pragmatic Sanction he hoped to have his daughter, Maria Theresa, succeed him.

RECOGNITION OF MARIA THERESA. Charles VI spent many years in having this Sanction recognized by his dominions and by the foreign countries. By making liberal concessions he persuaded all the important powers to respect and guarantee the Pragmatic Sanction. Upon the death of Charles VI (1740) Maria Theresa inherited his heterogeneous, ill-organized dominions.

EMERGENCE OF PRUSSIA

The Hohenzollerns, who had risen to the Electorate of Brandenburg, were the second most powerful family in the Germanies at this time. In the eighteenth century they made their state a first-rank power.

Rise of the Hohenzollerns. The Hohenzollerns were not important until they were given the Electorate of Brandenburg (1415) by the Emperor. In this frontier province the perpetual warfare with the Slavs gave them military experience. They accepted Lutheranism and proceeded to confiscate valuable property of the Catholic Church. Brandenburg became the leading Protestant state of Germany, just as Austria was the Catholic one. By marriages just prior to the Thirty Years' War, the Hohenzollerns secured the duchies of Cleves and of East Prussia. At the end of the war they got the bishoprics of Halberstadt, Minden, and Magdeburg and half of Pomerania.

Frederick William (1640-1688). Under the Great Elector, Frederick William (1640-1688), Brandenburg became an important force not only in the Germanies but in Europe as well.

FOREIGN AGGRANDIZEMENT. Frederick William obtained concessions at the Peace of Westphalia which increased his territories. Later, in a war between Sweden and Poland, he so cleverly carried on his double alliance as to have Poland renounce all claims to East Prussia and give him complete control. He further established the prestige of Brandenburg in the Dutch War (1672-1678) and showed Sweden that here was a rival for Baltic supremacy.

DOMESTIC POLICY. His domestic reforms were as successful and as important as his foreign. In the first place he consolidated Brandenburg, Cleves, and East Prussia into a centralized state with financial control in his own person. He established a national army. He encouraged industry and agriculture. When the Huguenots fled from France after the revocation of the Edict of Nantes, he invited them to settle in Brandenburg, and over 20,000 settled around Berlin.

Kingdom of Prussia (1701). The unified Brandenburg was recognized by the Emperor Leopold as a kingdom in 1701, in order to get its support in the War of the Spanish Succession, and in 1713 the other powers recognized it as the Kingdom of Prussia. Prussia was independent; Brandenburg had been a member of the Holy Roman Empire.

REFORMS OF FREDERICK WILLIAM I. King Frederick William I (1713-1740), the grandson of the Great Elector, was intent on increasing Prussia's prestige. He further developed absolutism and an effective army. By the closest economies he built the army up from 38,000 to 80,000 men without greatly increasing the burden of taxation and developed a great fighting machine. He continued the centralization of administration, and his "general directory" conducted finances and instituted a civil service system. Elementary education was made compulsory.

FREDERICK THE GREAT AND MARIA THERESA. In 1740, the year that Frederick the Great (Frederick II) came to the throne of Prussia, Maria Theresa became head of the Hapsburg dominions in Austria.

OTHER IMPORTANT GERMAN STATES

Bavaria. Bavaria on the upper Danube had been ruled for centuries by the Wittelsbach family. Maximilian I (1591-1651) had headed the Catholic League in the Thirty Years' War and at the Peace of Westphalia had gained territory which was formerly a part of the Palatinate. Despite the bond of a common religion and her proximity to Austria, Bavaria did not support her neighbor in the War of Spanish Succession, and in 1740 she allied herself with Prussia and France to dismember Austria.

Saxony. Saxony was the geographical center of the Germanies. Other factors which made it important were (a) that the ruling family of Wettins were imperial electors, (b) that it was a leading Lutheran state, and (c) that the Saxon dialect had become the literary language of Germany largely through the influence of Luther's translation of the Bible. Saxony might have become the leading state instead of Brandenburg, but its rulers were weak and allied themselves with Austria.

Hanover. Hanover was located in northwestern Germany and was also an electorate. Its first elector became George I of Great Britain (1714). Both George I and George II preferred Hanover to England as a place of residence, and they protected it against the Hapsburgs and Hohenzollerns. This personal union of Hanover and England lasted over one hundred years.

WARS OF FREDERICK II AND MARIA THERESA

Plan to Dismember Austria. After the death of Charles VI, Frederick II with France and Bavaria sought to dismember Maria Theresa's realm, thus cynically violating the previous agreement of all three states to respect the Pragmatic Sanction. The Elector of Bavaria was to be made Holy Roman Emperor; Prussia was to get Silesia; and France, the Austrian Netherlands.

War of Austrian Succession (1740-1748). The War of the Austrian Succession (1740-1748) got under way when Frederick II marched his troops into Silesia and claimed the duchy (cf. page 68). Maria Theresa, being pressed by a French and Bavarian army from the west, asked help of Magyars, Hungarians, Austrians, and Bohemians. Great Britain, anxious to prevent France from getting the Austrian Netherlands, joined with Austria; Spain supported France.

Course of War. Frederick II managed to keep control of Silesia until 1745, when Austria was forced to cede it to Prussia in order to concentrate her forces against the western allies. Obtaining Silesia, Frederick II withdrew from the war. Austria now proceeded to force back the French and Bavarians until Bavaria was conquered and the French had recrossed the Rhine. The war came to an end with the Treaty of Aix-la-Chapelle (1748).

Treaty of Aix-la-Chapelle (1748). The Treaty of Aix-la-Chapelle gave Silesia to Frederick II and reëstablished essentially the status quo which existed before the war for the other countries. The war was only a preliminary between Austria and Prussia for German leadership and between England and France for colonial and commercial supremacy.

"Diplomatic Revolution." Maria Theresa set about to recoup her losses and to recover her prestige by humbling Frederick II. She concentrated her efforts on improving the internal conditions of the country and in forming a coalition against Frederick II. She secured Saxony and Russia as allies and counted on the friendly attitude of Great Britain and Holland. The clever Kaunitz (Austrian Minister) maneuvered the French into joining the coalition against Frederick II. However, the war in America between France and England, which was renewed in 1754, caused England to form a definite alliance with Prussia. The alliance of France with Austria and of England with Prussia is known as the "Diplomatic Revolution."

Seven Years' War (1756-1763). The Seven Years' War (1756-1763) was the greatest war which the modern world had seen up to that time (cf. page 68). Its battle ground was Europe, India, and America.

COURSE OF WAR. Frederick immediately overran Saxony. Revealing his military genius, he outwitted the Austrians and their allies and completely defeated the French at Rossbach (1757) and the Austrians at Leuthen. But these victories did Frederick little good against the overwhelming coalition of his enemies. During the next five years Frederick was constantly on the defensive and was reduced to the most desperate straits. He derived some cheer from the French defeats in Hanover at the hands of the Prussian General Brunswick. The French finally had to appeal to the Spanish Bourbons for help, and a defensive alliance was formed among the Bourbon states of France, Spain, and the two Sicilies. Russia offered the real menace to Frederick. By 1759 the Russians had penetrated Brandenburg and captured Berlin. The death of Tsarina Elizabeth (1762) and the ascension of Peter III, an admirer of Frederick, resulted in the Russians deserting Maria Theresa, forming an alliance with Frederick, and returning the conquests which they had made. This astonishing piece of good luck saved Frederick II.

TREATIES OF HUBERTUSBURG AND PARIS (1763). The Treaty of Hubertusburg (1763) ended the conflict in Europe. Maria Theresa surrendered all claims to Silesia. Prussia and the Hohenzollerns were now the leaders in the Germanies. The Peace of Paris closed the war among Great Britain, France, and Spain.

Partition of Poland. Frederick the Great now sought to strengthen and consolidate Prussia. To prevent Austria from getting the upper hand, he entered into a strong alliance with Russia. As a result Frederick joined with Catherine of Russia in the first partition of Poland (1772). Russia took the country east of the Duna and Dnieper, while Frederick took West Prussia (except Danzig and Thorn), thereby linking Brandenburg and Prussia together. Austria also took a slice—Galicia. However, the partition was more favorable to Prussia than Austria. Further partitions of Poland occurred in 1793 and 1795 (see Chapter XII).

Significant Dates

Battle of Poltava	1709
Treaties of Stockholm	1719-1720
Second Partitition of Poland	1793
Third Partitition of Poland	1795

CHAPTER XII.

RUSSIA UNDER PETER THE GREAT AND CATHERINE II

RUSSIA OF THE SEVENTEENTH CENTURY

Extent of Russia. During the sixteenth and seventeenth centuries, with no barriers to their migrations, the Russian people expanded to take in the whole great area from Europe to the Pacific Ocean. The great rivers aided rather than hindered this expansion. For protection, there sprang up a semi-military group known as the Cossacks. As the people took in new lands, the power of the tsar extended with them.

Oriental Russia. The Russia of this period was Oriental, not Occidental. It obtained its religion from the Greek Church at Constantinople; habits and customs were colored by close association with the Mongols of Asia. The topography of the country tended to encourage agricultural pursuits and to cause emigration eastward. The lack of a port on the Baltic retarded Russian economic and political growth. Russia needed to become Westernized and to diminish the power of her strong neighbors—Sweden, Poland, and Turkey—before becoming a first-rate power in Europe.

Accession of Romanovs. After the direct line of Ivan the Great died out, Russia was a hotbed of civil wars, anarchy, and foreign intervention. Swedes, Poles, and Turks all harassed the country. Finally, a national assembly met at Moscow (1613) to elect a tsar. Michael Romanov was elected. He quickly reëstablished order at home, resisted foreign encroachments, and recovered Novgorod from the Swedes.

PETER THE GREAT (1682-1725)

Europeanization of Russia. Peter the Great traveled extensively in European countries with his special commission for enlisting European aid against the Turks. But during these travels he learned much about Western civilization and from time to time sent skilled workmen to Russia to instruct his people.

ABSOLUTISM UNDER PETER THE GREAT. Peter was an absolute monarch. Forced to hurry home because of a mutiny in his bodyguard, the Streltse, he severely punished the mutineers, killing several thousand. He then reorganized the army and made it a potent factor. Next he made the Church subordinate to the State by creating the Holy Synod, whose members he appointed. The government was remodeled along autocratic lines, and all traces of local·self-government were done away with.

INTRODUCTION OF OCCIDENTAL CUSTOMS. Western clothes and manners were forced upon the people. The Oriental semi-seclusion of women was prohibited. Peter also tried to improve economic conditions by improving agriculture.

Peter's Foreign Policy. The foreign aims of Peter were not only to extend the Russian dominions around the Caspian Sea towards Persia but also to obtain outlets to the Black and Baltic Seas. To gain his ends he had to engage in a conflict with ʻʻboth Turkey and Sweden.

CONFLICT WITH SWEDEN. Peter the Great was able partially to fulfill his foreign policy at the expense of Sweden which at Peter's accession was supreme in the Baltic.

Sweden controlled the countries of the Baltic in the seventeenth century. Denmark, Poland, and Brandenburg had tried to break up this monopoly without success. The rise of Prussia augured ill for Sweden's continued power. The neglect of economic development within the dominions by the sovereigns and their continued petty, but expensive, wars helped her decline.

The accession of the fifteen-year-old Charles XII (1697-1717) to the Swedish throne was the signal for the hostile European powers to plan the partition of the Baltic dominions of Sweden. The plan for this partition was that Russia would get Ingria and Karelia (port on the Baltic); Poland was to recover Livonia and annex Esthonia; Brandenburg was to occupy western Pomerania, and Denmark was to take Holstein and control the mouths of the Weser and Elbe Rivers. Brandenburg decided not to take part in the partition, but the others signed the alliance in 1699.

The Great Northern War (1699-1721) was no easy task for the allies. Charles XII proved to be a military genius of the first rank, and few historical spectacles are more amazing than the career of conquest which he now entered upon as the head of a state without a tenth of the resources of his enemies. First he defeated Denmark and made her sign a treaty in 1700. Next he took Warsaw and Cracow in Poland and made the Polish Diet accept his candidate for their king (Stanislaus Leszcznski, 1704). In the districts which he conquered in Russia, Saxony, and Poland he cruelly suppressed the people. Charles XII refused to sign an advantageous peace at this stage, and the great battle of Poltava (1709) followed, in which Peter the Great's reorganized army completely defeated the Swedes. Charles XII fled to Turkey and tried to stir up the Turks against Peter, but Peter bought them off by returning the town of Azov, which he had captured in 1696 from the Turks. The war dragged on, and Charles XII returned to invade Norway and to direct, but without avail, a last effort against the coalition now strengthened by Great Britain, Hanover, and Prussia. Charles lost his life in this invasion.

By the Treaties of Stockholm (1719-1720) Sweden became a third rate power; Denmark received Holstein; Hanover obtained the mouths of the Elbe and Weser Rivers; Prussia got the mouth of the Oder; and the cities of Stellia and Stettin were given to Poland under the restored Augustus of Saxony. The commercial heirs of Sweden were Great Britain, Denmark, and Prussia. The

Treaty of Nystad (1721) gave Russia not only the much sought Karelia and Ingria but also Esthonia and Livonia and a narrow strip of Southern Finland including the fortress of Viborg. Peter had finally secured his coveted "window" to the west. It remained for Catherine the Great to open up the Black Sea.

CATHERINE II (1762-1796)

Catherine II (1762-1796) carried on the work of Peter the Great by humbling Turkey and Poland, the two countries which prevented the expansion of Russia.

Domestic Policy of Catherine II. Catherine II was a Protestant German Princess who had married the heir to the Russian throne. She immediately made herself Russian, and after her husband had ruled less than a year she did away with him (Peter III) and became ruler herself. She centralized the administrative system of Russia by dividing the country into divisions and subdivisions with governors and vice-governors responsible to the central authority. She further subordinated the church by secularizing church property. She patronized literature and learning. Many of the foremost intellectuals of Europe gathered at her court.

Partitions of Poland. The weaknesses of Poland were (1) its lack of natural boundaries, (2) its heterogeneous population, (3) its varied religions, (4) its lack of an influential middle class between the haughty nobles and the oppressed, ignorant peasants, and (5) its ineffective government—the elective king was the puppet of European powers and the Diet could not enact laws without a unanimous vote (*liberum veto*). Catherine II recognized these weaknesses and upon the death of Augustus III, with the help of Frederick of Prussia she had her own candidate, Stanislaus Poniatowski, elected as king. Even though engaged in a conflict with Turkey, Catherine II was on hand to join with Austria and Prussia in the first partition of Poland (1772). Russia got all the land east of the Dnieper and Duna Rivers, while Prussia got West Prussia except Danzig, and Austria took Galicia and the city of Cracow. Efforts of Poland to remedy its political situation were thwarted, and in 1793 Russia took additional territory. Two years later (1795) Austria once more joined with them and completed the work of erasing an independent Poland from the map. As a result of these partitions Austria got the upper valley of the Vistula, Prussia the lower valley including Warsaw, and Russia the rest—the lion's share. The modern Poland was a post-World War creation.

Catherine II and Turkey. While having her eyes on Poland, Catherine the Great was still desirous of getting a "window" in the Black Sea. Trouble with Turkey was inevitable. The Turks had long threatened Christian Western Europe, but in the seventeenth century their power started to decline. They lost Hungary to the Austrian Hapsburgs, the boundary of Poland was extended to the Dneister River and the trading centers on the Dalmatian and Greek coasts were given to the Venetians. The Turks were unable to hold their possessions because of (1) the character of the Turkish life, (2) the decline of their once great military machine, and (3) corruption in the government. The Turkish War (1768-1774) was caused by the fear of the Turks that Russia would annex Poland, and by France, who encouraged the Turks to fight against Russia. Russia easily over-ran Moldavia and Wallachia, captured Azov, and caused the Greeks to revolt against the Sultan. The Turks consented to the Treaty of Kuchuk Kainarji (1774) by which (1) Turkey gave up Azov and renounced all claims to land north of the Black Sea, (2) Turkey recovered Wallachia, Moldavia, and Greece on condition that they be governed better, (3) Russia obtained the right to free navigation in Turkish waters, and (4) Russia was recognized as the protector of certain churches in the city of Constantinople. Through these provisions Russia was able to control the principalities on the northern coast of the Black Sea, and Catherine had been successful in getting her "window" in the Black Sea region.

Significant Dates

Diderot's *Encyclopedia* . 1751-1765

Failure of Turgot's Reform
    Efforts 1774-1776

Smith's *Wealth of Nations* . . 1776

Joseph II, Enlightened
    Despot 1780-1790

CHAPTER XIII.

OLD RÉGIME

MEANING OF THE OLD RÉGIME

By the Old Régime is meant the whole European political and social organization as it existed before the French Revolution of 1789. The French Revolution and the Napoleonic Wars that followed so entirely transformed these old institutions and introduced so many new dominant forces that it seems appropriate to give a special name to the old order. The Old Régime was associated with feudalism—its inequalities based upon the theory of privileged and non-privileged classes,—absolutism in government as well as corruption in political and religious organizations, and the concentration of land and wealth.

Great Britain. In Chapter VI the English revolutions resulting in the supremacy of Parliament were traced. The English system of constitutional government that was thus established was unique in Europe in the eighteenth century and was looked upon by many political thinkers on the continent as an excellent solution of the problem of government. Great Britain was regarded as the country of freedom. This freedom of Britain was based not only upon the Parliamentary supremacy but on the tradition of legal rights of the individual.

89

PLACE OF KING. The King of England was fast becoming a mere figure-head, for during the seventeenth century he had been deprived of his power to lay taxes, to make or prevent laws, to control the judiciary, or to maintain a standing army against the will of Parliament.

PARLIAMENT, REPRESENTATIVE BODY. The real power in England was the Parliament which had taken over the powers that the king lost. However, the majority of the people had no voice in the choice of these representatives because of the restrictions of suffrage, the unequal apportionment of representation, and the presence of wide-spread corruption. Instead, a small group of great landed families maintained a practical monopoly of Parliamentary seats.

CABINET IN ENGLAND. The Cabinet system was firmly established at the time of George I and Sir Robert Walpole, (see Chapter VI). It determined the legislation to be presented to Parliament, and when its policy was refused, it resigned as a unit. With the cabinet responsible to the House of Commons, the king became a mere ceremonial head. Under George III, who ascended the throne in 1760, there was a considerable recovery of the influence of the king in the government, but the failure of Lord North, Prime Minister under George III, to control Parliament—and particularly his failure in the American War—served as an impetus for reform.

AGITATION FOR FURTHER REFORMS. The reform movement (Chartism) which demanded an extension of suffrage, proportionate representation, payment of members of Parliament, reduction of property qualifications for members of Parliament, adoption of the secret ballot, and annual Parliaments was furthered by Charles Fox and William Pitt, the Younger. Pitt, who became Prime Minister in 1784, was all ready to place reform programs before Parliament, but the rumblings from the coming French Revolutions frightened him and his associates. They were afraid that revolution might break out in England, and so they turned about and repressed all agitation for reform.

Divine Right Monarchy in France. The part played by France in destroying the Old Régime gives a special importance to the study of the French government during the eighteenth century. The government of France was an absolute, divine-right monarchy.

PLACE OF KING. Louis XV (1715-1774) was the king; he was also the government. He was aided in the administration of government by a Royal Council composed of a small group who supervised the affairs of the kingdom. The local representatives of the royal council were the bailiffs, seneschals, governors, and intendants. The intendants had a great deal of power, such as the fixing of the amount of taxation a district must pay, the supervision of police, the recruiting of the army, the building of roads, and relieving the poor. There were a few instruments of administration that maintained a partial independence of the king. The Parlement of Paris was the supreme court which registered royal decrees. It occasionally showed signs of resisting the king's arbitrary will, but such opposition was ineffective down to the year 1788. Some of the provinces had provincial "Estates" or assemblies. The towns were governed by town councils whose duties greatly overlapped those of the intendants.

POLITICAL AND SOCIAL INEQUALITIES. The whole administrative system was one of confusion and corruption: government officials were skillful grafters; there was no uniformity of law or justice. In one place the old Roman Law was retained, and in another the Germanic Law was enforced. Arbitrary imprisonment under the notorious system of *lettres de cachet* was common. The courts were presided over by judges, "noblesse de la robe," who bought their positions outright from the king. In the army, one had to be a noble to become an officer; the ranks were made up of unwilling peasants and foreign mercenaries. Financial corruption threatened the very existence of the French monarchy; no record of the income and outgo was kept; the burdens of taxation were not distributed over all the people but fell hardest on the unprivileged classes—peasants and bourgeoisie. The custom of farming the taxes—sale of the privilege of tax collection to private speculators—introduced an additional element of injustice.

LOUIS XV AT VERSAILLES. Louis XV preferred to spend his time with his mistresses, gambling or hunting, rather than with the affairs of state. But the gayety of Versailles did not blot out the misery of France, and criticism was loud and strong. Attempts, however, to suppress agitation failed miserably and Louis managed to prevent the "deluge" while he lived.

FAILURE OF ABSOLUTISM UNDER LOUIS XVI. Louis XVI (1774-1792), grandson of Louis XV, was content at first to allow his ministers to govern. He partially understood the crying need for reform and was honestly anxious for the welfare of his people. To this end he appointed the liberal economist Turgot as minister of finance. Turgot attempted to reform the finances, break up the restricting gild system that strangled trade, and introduce strict economy in the government, but his desire to tax the privileged classes caused dissension, and he was dismissed in 1776. Jacques Necker succeeded Turgot as Minister of Finance. Necker's publication of the *Compte Rendu* or report on the financial condition caused his downfall in 1781. The *Compte Rendu* and Necker's attempt to check the extravagant granting of pensions to favorites offended powerful persons at court, particularly the Queen, Marie Antoinette. The cost of aiding the American colonies in their War of Independence further embarrassed the French financially. The only possible remedy was reform of taxation along the lines that had been suggested by Turgot, but the opposition of the nobles and clergy to any interference with their exemption privileges was adamant, and Louis XVI was not the man to break tradition in accordance with public necessity. He continued to drift along, hoping for a financial miracle. Finally the king admitted that he could not handle the situation alone and called an Assemble of Notables (1787), in the hope that they would consent to being taxed, but they suggested that the problem of taxation be referred to the Estates General, the old representative body which had not met since 1614. This act spelled the doom of absolutism in France.

CONDITION OF THE PEASANTS

Primitive Farming. Still widely used were old implements and methods. Scientific farming had hardly begun. In some places prosperous farmers broke away from the old way and experimented with different crops and fertilizers, but the vast majority continued with old methods.

Remains of Feudalism. The people still lived under a semi-feudal system. Some serfdom was still to be found in all countries except England. The peasants had no voice in the government. They had to pay heavy taxes to lord, king, and church— corvée (enforced labor on the public roads), tailles (land tax), and tithes (tenths to church), and many had other feudal obligations. The condition of the peasants was deplorable. Their food was scarce, unvaried, and coarse; their shelter was not only humble but unsanitary, and their clothing was inadequate. If by hard work and self-denial a peasant succeeded in accumulating a small saving, he was as likely as not to be virtually robbed of it by the tax collector. The condition of the peasant was worst in eastern Europe, particularly Russia, Poland, and Hungary, and best in England. In France conditions were bad, but the peasant was more alert to his situation and more hopeful of reform.

BOURGEOISIE

Growth of Cities. Towns developed fast during the seventeenth and eighteenth centuries, so that by 1787 there were eighty towns with over 10,000 inhabitants. The growth of cities was given great impetus by the colonial expansion of the seventeenth and eighteenth centuries. London was the largest with over a million; Paris had 500,000 and Amsterdam, Hamburg, Bremen, and Frankfurt were large prosperous trading centers.

Development of Industry. The industries of the eighteenth century had greatly increased in quantity and variety since the Middle Ages and now not only produced for home consumption but also for other markets. This growth had occurred in spite of many obstacles. The gild system still held sway over the different industries on the continent, but in England it had been broken down. Initiative, invention, and improved methods were opposed by the gilds. Government regulation also served to impede rather than accelerate industry, in spite of the efforts of such men as Colbert who tried not only to regulate, but also to encourage new industries.

Commerce in Eighteenth Century. Commerce, likewise, was hindered because of poor methods of transportation and governmental restrictions. Chartered companies like the East India

Company, Dutch East India Company, and the Hudson Bay Company monopolized the colonial trade. However, commerce grew and the products of the new world and "The Indies" were laid at Europe's feet.

Rise of Bourgeoisie. One of the most important results of the development of commerce and industry was the rise of the bourgeoisie—the middle class of merchants, workers, wholesalers, gild-masters, and shop keepers. The bourgeoisie were strongest in England and France. Once this group had obtained wealth and learning they clamored for power—political power. The bourgeoisie of England had been able to gain some representation in Parliament, and now the same class in France was clamoring for recognition in the government.

PRIVILEGED CLASSES

The privileged classes in Europe were the higher clergy and the nobility (First and Second Estates, as they were called in France and in some other countries) and made up only one per cent of all the people. (Although technically belonging to the First Estate, many of the lower clergy were poor, hard-working, and mentally more identified with the unprivileged classes than with their own order). These two groups were distinguished from the rest of the people by rank, hereditary landed property, and privileges.

First Estate. The Higher Clergy was in a sorry state of corruption. Dissipated nobles had obtained church offices and used them as a source of revenue instead of spiritual leadership. Meanwhile the Lower Clergy was having a difficult time in getting enough to live on and to attend to the needs of the parish.

Second Estate. The Higher Nobility was merely ornan.ental. They spent their time at the royal court in a life of ease and enjoyment, while their estates were controlled by close-fisted agents whose object was to get as much as possible from the peasants. The poorer nobles (Country Gentry) could not afford such a life and so remained on their estates.

RELIGION

Christianity at this time was not propagated by the Roman Catholic Church alone but also by the Anglican and other Protestant churches.

Roman Catholic Church in Eighteenth Century. The Roman Catholic Church was still the greatest and most powerful church, having retained its hold on Italy, Spain, Portugal, France, the Austrian Netherlands, Bavaria, Poland, and several Swiss Cantons, to say nothing of large portions of Bohemia, Hungary, and Ireland. The Orthodox Roman Catholics did not compromise with other sects but held strongly to their beliefs and looked to the secular and regular clergy for guidance. But the Catholic Church had lost much of its power. The rulers of Protestant countries came to look upon the Pope as a mere rival prince. Profession of the Catholic religion in these countries was made difficult by persecution and the denial of political rights. In Roman Catholic countries the king had been able to obtain the privilege of appointing high church officers. The state courts had superseded the ecclesiastical courts in most cases (except blasphemy, contempt of religion, and heresy). However, the church was the leader in education; marriages were performed by the church and the suppression of heresies was in its hands. The unity of the church was impaired by a number of internal movements. Jansenism, started by a Flemish bishop Cornelius Jansen (1585-1638) was a religious revival akin in some respects to Protestantism. It stressed the necessity of conversion and attacked the excessive formalism and dependence on ceremonial that characterized many theologians. Jansenism was attacked by the Jesuits and was ultimately adjudged heretical in the famous bull "Unigenitus" (1713). Another dissension, Febronianism, questioned the right of the Pope to interfere with temporal rulers and maintained that the general council of bishops was superior to the Pope. The Jesuits, who opposed Febronianism, were called Ultramontanists. The Jesuits had become famous as educators, preachers, and missionaries, but their interference in state affairs, the abuse of their power and wealth, and the laxity of some of their members led to their suppression by papal decree (1773).

Church of England in Eighteenth Century. The Anglican Church of England occupied a place of privilege and great wealth in the British Isles (except Scotland). The Toleration Act (1689) had made it a little easier for Protestant Dissenters, but they could not hold political offices without special permission of Parliament. Baptism, registration of births, deaths and marriages could be performed only by Anglican clergymen. The Roman Catholics in England had practically no religious, political, or civil rights. In Ireland, although Catholics were in the immense numerical majority, they were forced to pay tithes to the Church of England. Besides the Presbyterians and Separatists, there were other dissenters in England. The Baptists were an off-shoot of the Separatists believing in adult baptism by immersion and in religious liberty. Another group, the Unitarians, who did not obtain religious liberty until 1844, denied the divinity of Christ. The Quakers, strong opponents of war and slavery, founded by George Fox (1624-1690), believed that true religion was accompanied by deep emotion and workings of the spirit. The Methodists became important under John Wesley (1703-1791).

Lutheranism in Eighteenth Century. On the continent Lutheranism was supreme in Denmark, Norway, Sweden, and several German states including Prussia, Saxony, and Brunswick. Presbyterian or Reformed Churches, which held that the Lord's Supper was merely commemorative and favored abolishing altar-lights, crucifixes, and set prayers, was the state religion in Scotland and the Dutch Netherlands, and had large support in France (Huguenots), Germany, and Switzerland.

Skepticism and Deism. The growth of skepticism regarding Christianity was greatest during the eighteenth century. The skeptics doubted the reliability of the Bible and the whole Christian Church. They believed in each man's determining his own religion and relation to God. One group became known as Deists. The Deists maintained a belief in a vague all-ruling "Providence," but rejected the personal God of Christian orthodoxy. Deism was influenced by the scientific and intellectual progress of the century.

AGE OF "ENLIGHTENMENT"

Eighteenth Century Scientists. Many great men worked in the field of science. Leaders experimented in different countries, hoping to find new knowledge. It was an age in which a thesis had to be proved before it would be accepted.

SIR ISAAC NEWTON (1642-1727). The greatest of all the scientists of the period was the Englishman, Sir Isaac Newton. His improved telescope facilitated the study of astronomy, but his discovery of the principle of gravitation and its expression in a mathematical formula was his most famous contribution. His *Philosophiae Naturalis Principia Mathematica,* usually called simply the *Principia,* ranks as one of the greatest scientific treatises of all time. It was published in 1687 and became almost an inspired Bible for the physicists, astronomers, and mathematicians of the eighteenth and nineteenth centuries.

GOTTFRIED WILHELM VON LEIBNITZ (1646-1716). Gottfried Wilhelm von Leibnitz, a German philosopher, shared with Newton the creation of a new branch of mathematics, the differential and integral calculus, which has greatly aided engineering.

BENJAMIN FRANKLIN (1706-1790). Benjamin Franklin invented the lightning rod after observing that lightning was merely an electric phenomenon. As one of the leaders of the American Revolution, Franklin was much admired in France, where he was regarded as one who "was able to restrain alike thunderbolts and tyrants."

JOSEPH PRIESTLEY (1733-1804). Joseph Priestley, Antoine Lavoisier (1743-1794), and Henry Cavendish (1731-1810) made beginnings in modern chemistry.

EDWARD JENNER (1749-1823). Edward Jenner, an English doctor, showed how smallpox could be prevented by vaccination.

SCIENTIFIC PATRONAGE. Everywhere the scientists were favored by the kings and nobles. Societies, such as the "Royal Society" of London (1662) and the "French Academy," where the latest discoveries and experiments were discussed, were founded during this period.

Dissemination of Knowledge by Rationalists. Knowledge was easily spread now that printing was well developed and there was plenty of it to disseminate. Characteristic of the eighteenth century was the movement toward rationalism and the criticism of political, social, and religious institutions.

JOHN LOCKE (1632-1704). In England, John Locke's ideas represent the rationalists' practical aims. Locke claimed that government should exist by consent of the governed, that education should be more wide-spread, that natural law should not give way to religious dogmas, and that all except atheists should have religious toleration.

FRANÇOIS VOLTAIRE (1694-1778). François Voltaire (François Arouet) was one of the foremost intellectual leaders of the period. His sarcasm earned him the pride and ire of the monarchs of France, Russia, and Prussia. He criticised the existing conditions in government, in society, and in the church. His greatest weakness was his inability to offer something constructive to take the place of what he would tear down.

DENIS DIDEROT (1713-1784). Denis Diderot is noted for editing the *Encyclopedia,* which not only attempted to summarize all knowledge, but also to express the ideas of its rationalist and deist contributors on religion, society, and science. The contributors to the *Encyclopedia* included most of the intellectual leaders of France. More than any other work or group the *Encyclopedia* and the "Encyclopedists" came to stand for the Age of Reason and Enlightenment.

MONTESQUIEU (1689-1755). Montesquieu, a French lawyer-nobleman, was noted for his works on government. *The Spirit of the Laws* (1744) was the written expression of his ideas.

JEAN JACQUES ROUSSEAU (1712-1778). Jean Jacques Rousseau was not primarily a rationalist, but he was one of the most influential writers of the times. Not reason but feeling was his idol. To Rousseau may be traced much of the reaction against reason that characterized the literary "Romantic Movement" of the late eighteenth and early nineteenth centuries. He suggested a plan of "Back to Nature" to take the place of society with all its evils. He greatly influenced education. In his *Social Contract* he demanded that the people have control of the government. His ideas were the inspiration for the early stages of the French Revolution.

BECCARIA (1738-1794). Beccaria, an Italian marquis, in his book on *Crimes and Punishments* (1764) attacked the old judicial methods and advocated milder methods.

ADAM SMITH (1723-1790). Adam Smith, a Scotchman, wrote a book, *The Wealth of Nations* (1776), in which he advocated a system of "laissez faire" in industry. Smith's book did more than any other single factor to break down mercantilism.

Enlightened Despots. The "enlightened" or "benevolent" despots of Prussia, Russia, and Austria were rulers who were paternalistic but not democratic. They represented a kind of compromise between the Old Régime and the new spirit. They were greatly influenced by the philosophers and scientists who characterized the "enlightened era."

FREDERICK II OF PRUSSIA (1740-1786). Frederick II of Prussia increased the power and prestige of his kingdom at the expense of his neighbors. He thought of his position as paternalistic and worked for the benefit of his subjects as he thought best. He reformed the system of justice, established elementary schools, allowed a certain amount of religious liberty and encouraged general prosperity. His army was the envy of all Europe. He was the most successful example of the theory of benevolent despotism.

CATHERINE II OF RUSSIA (1762-1796). In Russia Catherine II posed as a liberal-minded ruler, but she had no sincere wish to improve the position of the peasants but rather to increase Russia's prestige among the other nations. She encouraged men of letters to visit her not only in Russia but from other countries for form's sake. She promised a constitution and emancipation of the serfs, but nothing came of her promises.

JOSEPH II OF AUSTRIA (1780-1790). The Holy Roman Emperor, Joseph II of Austria (1765-1790), was not only the most enthusiastic but also the most unsuccessful of the benevolent despots. Unlike Maria Theresa, his mother, he was neither a devout Roman Catholic nor a practical ruler. He was an admirer of the French philosophers from whom he had imbibed many liberal ideas. He set about to institute wholesale reforms regardless of prejudice, of tradition, or of custom. His attempts to extend his possessions, to abolish local liberty in administration of government and class distinction, all ended in dismal failure. He aroused the bitter antagonism of his nobility, while even the peasants, for whom he thought he was acting, were unappreciative of his efforts.

┌
│ *Significant Dates*

Estates General Convened . 1789

Fall of the Bastille 1789

French Victory at Valmy . 1792

Execution of Louis XVI . . 1793

"Reign of Terror" . . 1793-1794
┘

CHAPTER XIV.

FRENCH REVOLUTION

SCOPE OF FRENCH REVOLUTION

The French Revolution was the process by which absolutism in France gave way to democracy, and class distinction gave way to social equality. In a larger sense the French Revolution was the whole European movement that began in France and spread through Europe during the Napoleonic period and that broke up the Old Régime. Through the nineteenth century the ideas and inspiration of the French Revolution continued to dominate politics. The great historical importance of the French Revolution lies in its character as a generator of world revolution, and in the power and persistence of its basic ideas. Like the Protestant Revolt two hundred and fifty years earlier, the French Revolution began an era of conflict of fundamental theories and interests—an era of conflict that has not yet worked itself out.

Estates General (1789). The feeling of unrest among the peasants, bourgeoisie, privileged classes, and royalty, which was caused by wide-spread economic distress and evidence everywhere that the system of the Old Régime was breaking down did not abate with the calling of the Estates General.

ORGANIZATION OF ESTATES GENERAL. The Estates General was made up of representatives of the clergy, nobles, and commoners—three estates each electing its own representatives by an indirect method. As a concession to popular demand Louis XVI had authorized the Third Estate to elect double their representation—there were as many Third Estate deputies as for the First and Second Estates combined. These were the pick of the Third Estate—lawyers, judges, and scholars. They were intent upon carrying out the reforms suggested by the "cahiers" (lists of grievances and suggested remedies). With Mirabeau (1749-1791), the young noble orator and radical, and with Sieyès (1748-1836), the tactful priest, who was more interested in politics than in religion, the Third Estate's prestige was greatly increased. When the Estates General convened in May, the King intended that it should solve the financial problems. Reform of the general government system was far from his thoughts. But the leaders of the Third Estate were determined on fundamental changes. To this end they demanded that voting should be done "by head" and that the Estates General should be organized into one body. Organization into a single body meant that the Third Estate would be able to control.

FORMATION OF NATIONAL ASSEMBLY (1789). When Louis XVI failed to decide the way in which the Estates General should be organized, the Third Estate proclaimed itself a National Assembly (June 17). On June 20 the members of the Assembly took the "Tennis Court Oath," swearing that they would not separate until they had drawn up a constitution for France. Louis XVI then attempted to make the Estates sit separately, but Mirabeau and the members of the Third Estate refused, challenging the King to use military force. The King finally reversed his decrees and issued another, which made the Estates General one house voting "by head." The Estates General now became the National Constituent Assembly.

PARIS SAVES ASSEMBLY. Louis XVI, now entirely under the influence of a reactionary court circle, attempted to overawe the Assembly by garrisoning troops around Paris and Versailles. The second dismissal of Necker, the popular financial minister, also aroused the Assembly and the people.

On July 14, 1789, in part because of the brilliant harangue of the journalist, Camille Desmoulins, the Parisian mob captured the Bastille. The royal control of Paris was shaken off and a new local government—the commune—was set up with elected representatives. Louis XVI hastily recalled Necker, appointed Lafayette (who, although a member of the nobility, was popular with the masses) commander of the newly formed National Guard, recognized the new Paris government, and accepted the new tricolor cockade—red, white, and blue. He also promised to curtail the activities of the royal troops.

Louis XVI may have had good intentions but he was dominated by the Queen, Marie Antoinette, and the Court. The coming of additional royal troops was the occasion for an extravagant party at Versailles. The belief that the Court was again plotting to overthrow the Assembly by force, and exaggerated reports of the party aroused the starving people of Paris. On October 5 a large group of the poorest women of Paris walked twelve miles to Versailles and demanded bread. That the royal pair might no longer plan and scheme unwatched, the King, Queen, and heir to the throne were forced to leave Versailles and accompany the people back to Paris. The National Assembly, which Paris had once more saved, was also removed to that city. After this removal the National Assembly felt increased security and confidence as the city was a hot-bed of revolutionary agitation.

While these events were happening, the Old Régime was crumbling. Uprisings in many of the country districts caused large numbers of the nobility to flee the country (émigrés), and their chateaux were burned. The intendants and governors left, and communes, with elected officials, were set up. Tax collections largely increased.

Constructive Work of National Constituent Assembly (1789-1791). The National Constituent Assembly not only brought about the end of the Old Régime but also set up in its place a limited monarchy with the supreme authority in the hands of the elected representatives of the nation. The work of this Assembly is the most constructive and vital of the whole era. It reflected the moderate reform sentiment of the bourgeoisie and the liberal sections of the nobility and clergy.

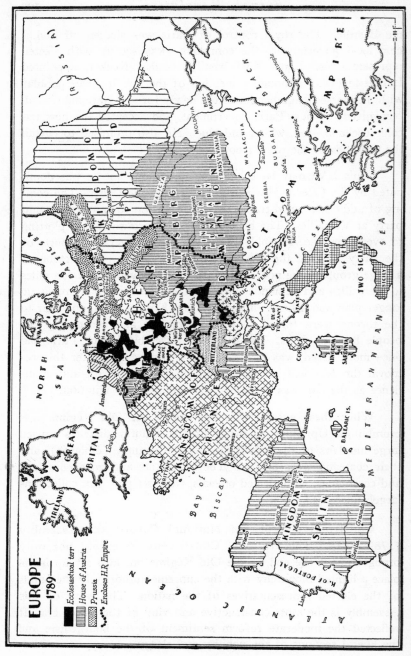

EUROPE
—1789—

Ecclesiastical terr.
House of Austria
Prussia
Encloses H.R.Empire

AUGUST DAYS. The abolition of feudalism and serfdom ended exemption from taxation, the special privileges of the nobles, the rights of the church to collect tithes, and the exclusive right of the nobility to hold office. Accomplished in the August Days (August 4-5), these changes rank paramount among the achievements of the National Assembly.

DECLARATION OF RIGHTS OF MAN (1789). The Declaration of the Rights of Man, which drew ideas from Great Britain's Magna Carta (1215) and Bill of Rights (1688) and from the American Declaration of Independence (1776), was even more a reflection of the new French spirit of "enlightenment" as exemplified by the Encyclopedists and Rousseau. Further, it was a statement of the principles of liberty, it defined certain civil and political rights, and it became the fighting creed of the French Revolution.

NEW ADMINISTRATIVE SYSTEM. The administrative system was completely reorganized, and the county was divided into districts, cantons, and communes. Local self-government was instituted. The judiciary was also reorganized and a modification of the law started.

NEW STATUS OF CLERGY. The financial strain was temporarily relieved at the expense of the clergy. The rich lands of the Catholic Church were seized and used as security for paper money (assignats). Not only was the property of the Church confiscated, but the clergy was made into a civil body, elected by the members of the parish according to the "Civil Constitution of the Clergy" (1790). The clergy was compelled to take an oath to the "Civil Constitution." However, the Pope forbade them to take it. Those who refused to take the oath were known as non-juring, whereas those that left the country were known as émigrés. As a result of this "Civil Constitution" the opposition of the Catholics to the Revolution was greatly increased. It stirred up desperate counter-revolutionary activity in many of the country districts and alienated the support of many liberals outside France.

CONSTITUTION OF 1791. Finally there was drawn up a constitution, the first written constitution in any large European country. The Constitution provided for the separation of the legislative, executive, and judicial powers. The executive power was theoretically vested in the king, but practically he had no powers. The legislative power was given to a unicameral Legislative Assembly, whose members were to be chosen by indirect elections. The chief weakness of the constitution was its paralysis of the executive power which arose from the distrust inspired by the King.

Problems Facing Legislative Assembly. The new Legislative Assembly, elected under the Constitution of 1791, met at Paris on October 1. From the first it was continually harassed by domestic and foreign disorders. Through a well-meant but unfortunate decision of the National Assembly, none of its members were eligible for election to the new Legislative Assembly, which was thus deprived of the talent and experience of the men who had made the constitution.

PARTY STRIFE. The Assembly was composed of many irreconcilable factions. A radical group, the "Mountain," demanded further reform, the abolition of the monarchy, and the establishment of a centralized, national republic. A moderate group, the Girondists, were willing to give the constitution a trial and favored a decentralized federal republic if it should prove necessary to abandon the limited monarchy. The more important radical leaders were Marat, the fiery newspaper editor; Danton, the orator; and Robespierre, the leader of the Jacobin Club. None of these three was a member of the Legislative Assembly, but their influence as agitators was exercised through their followers. Besides the radicals, the King tried to interfere with the work of the assembly, the peasants revolted in the Vendée, and the émigrés were busy trying to discredit the legislative body.

FOREIGN DANGER. Foreign hostility to the revolution did not crystallize until it was apparent that the reformers intended to shake the political and social foundations from their roots, all over Europe. Great Britain looked with alarm upon the events in France. But the first champion of European opposition to the revolution was the Holy Roman Emperor, Leopold II, brother of Marie Antoinette. With Frederick William II of Prussia,

Leopold issued the Declaration of Pillnitz (1791), declaring that the return of order and of monarchy to France was an object of "common interest to all sovereigns of Europe."

WAR SENTIMENT. There were three different groups in France that favored a foreign war. Marie Antoinette and her circle favored a war because a victory for France would increase the prestige of the royalty; in defeat, absolutism would undoubtedly be restored by the enemy. The Constitutionalists (Bourgeoisie), under Lafayette, believed that war would consolidate France. Finally, the Radicals wanted war so that they could stir up the whole of Europe, obtain a republic for France, and assure the triumph of democracy throughout Europe.

INVASION REPULSED. The Girondists and Feuillants got control of the Assembly and forced Louis XVI to declare war on Austria and Prussia in April, 1792. At first the ill-organized armies of the French were no match for the superior forces of the enemy under the Duke of Brunswick plus the intrigue of the French royal family. The Proclamation of the Duke of Brunswick (July, 1792) failed in its intention of terrifying the revolutionary party but caused instead the insurrection of August 9-10, in which the Paris mob murdered the Swiss Guards and forced the deputies to suspend the King. This date marks the end of the Legislative Assembly's control of the situation. A new Paris Commune, under the effective control of Danton and Robespierre, became the real power of the government. The election of a National Convention based upon universal manhood suffrage was authorized. Before this Convention could be elected and meet, rumors of the advance of the foreign armies into France spread a panic. The desperate emergency seemed to justify any atrocity. In a wild uprising known as the September Massacres, thousands of royalists were killed. Dumouriez succeeded Lafayette, who had surrendered to the allies, as leader of the French army, and he won his first victory at Valmy (September 20, 1792). After Valmy, the French easily turned back the Austrians and Prussians.

National Convention and First French Republic (1792-1795). The National Convention met on the day after the victory of Valmy, and immediately voted to abolish the monarchy and establish the First French Republic. The National Convention not only brought the foreign war to a successful completion but also constructed a republican form of government in France.

FACTIONS IN NATIONAL CONVENTION. The National Convention was made up of the Girondists, now the extreme "right" party, with their leaders Brissot, Vergniaud, Roland, and Condorcet; the Mountainists (Jacobins) with their leaders Danton, Robespierre, and Carnot; and the Plain, which made up a majority of the house, but the members of which were in general vacillators, anxious to be with the winners.

EXECUTION OF LOUIS XVI. The first act of the National Convention was to dispose of the King by having him beheaded (January 21, 1793) after finding him guilty of plotting against the government. The Girondists opposed the execution of the King, and their loss of the crucial test vote on this issue marked the end of their leadership in the Convention.

DISSOLUTION OF FIRST COALITION. The foreign foes were turned back, and France posed as the deliverer of mankind from the evils of the old régime in all Europe. But her strength led the countries of Europe to form the First Coalition against France in 1793. She rallied against her foes, and with the military genius of Carnot and with new generals in training, won a series of victories resulting in the break up of the First Coalition in 1795.

"REIGN OF TERROR." A strong central government was organized with the Committee of Public Safety as the core. From 1793-1794 this committee instituted a "reign of terror" in which thousands were guillotined because they were "suspects." In this manner most of the foes of the National Convention within France were done away with. Among the leaders who were guillotined were Marie Antoinette, Brissot, Vergniaud, Danton, Desmoulins, St. Just, and finally Robespierre. The death of Robespierre ended the "reign of terror."

DOMESTIC REFORMS OF NATIONAL CONVENTION. The work of the National Convention in furthering the earlier social reforms which were started was to some extent helpful. It sought to reduce inequalities of wealth by fostering the sale of land to the poor and by regulating prices. A new calendar, dating from September 22, 1792, was adopted. Permanent reforms were made, such as (a) establishing a uniform system of weights and measures based on the metric system, (b) establishing the basis of a system of state education, (c) separating the church and state, and (d) preparing a single code of laws. Unfortunately the violence of the reign of terror tended to obscure and cast discredit on these real achievements. To most of Europe the National Convention represented mere anarchy. "Jacobinism" and "democracy" became fighting words like "communism" or "fascism" today.

CONSTITUTION OF 1795. The Constitution of the Year III provided for a bicameral legislature and an executive which was to be composed of five men, called Directors, who were to supervise laws and appoint ministers of state. The Electorate was made up of taxpayers who had lived at least a year in one place. This Constitution represented a reaction from Jacobin ideas of pure democracy, and the establishment of bourgeois liberalism.

Directory (1795-1799). The period of the Directory was brought to an end because internal difficulties made it easy for an ambitious general to overthrow mediocre directors and to set himself up as a dictator.

WEAKNESSES UNDER DIRECTORY. The Directory, which was not made up of great leaders but only of average men, could not cope with the situation. The ablest political leaders had either been purged during the reign of terror or had been driven out of the country. The Directors did manage to check the reactionaries and the radicals in the assembly, but only by the use of violence and corruption. The financial difficulties once more promised to ruin the country. The assignats had steadily decreased in value because of their frequent issuance. In 1797 they were demonetized. The interest on two-thirds of the debt was suspended.

NAPOLEON BONAPARTE (1796-1800). Napoleon Bonaparte was appointed to command the army in Italy. In one year he controlled northern Italy, having completely defeated the Austrians and Sardinians. By the Treaty of Campo Formio, Austria gave France the Austrian Netherlands and the Ionian Islands. Bonaparte enjoyed great popular fame for his successes. In 1798 he set out on his Egyptian Expedition and in his absence Great Britain, Austria, and Russia formed the Second Coalition because of the Directory's attempt to set up republics on the French model in the small adjacent countries. The French were continually defeated; the newly made republics collapsed; and when Napoleon returned he was greeted as the "man of the hour." Within a month he had overthrown the corrupt and incompetent Directory and created a new constitution (1799) making himself First Consul of the Republic with practically unlimited personal power. The success of militarism and the downfall of democracy at the hands of Napoleon marks the end of the Revolution proper.

"Liberté, Égalité, Fraternité." The true significance of the French Revolution in its historic rôle as the modernizer of Europe is found in the three words "Liberté, Égalité, and Fraternité" or Liberty, Equality, and Fraternity.

LIBERTÉ. Liberty in 1789 meant the fulfillment of certain political and civil ideals—a guarantee of personal rights. It was embodied in the Declaration of the Rights of Man.

ÉGALITÉ. Equality meant the end of privilege and the recognition of the equality of men before the law.

FRATERNITÉ. Fraternity stood for a feeling of brotherhood among all those who wished to improve the lot of man. It also stood for the growing spirit of national solidarity or patriotism.

CHAPTER XV.

NAPOLEONIC ERA

NAPOLEON BONAPARTE

From 1800 to 1815 one man held the center of the European stage. Coming to the head of affairs in a France stirred to its depths by the tremendous upheaval of the Revolution, Napoleon Bonaparte was able for fifteen years to direct the immense energy of the Revolution to the service of his personal ambition. For about ten years he met with continual success and displayed a combination of military and administrative genius such as has probably never been equalled. In the end he was destroyed by the same force that had raised him to the height of power—the force of national patriotism, that from 1800 to 1808 made the armies of France invincible, but from 1808 to 1815 raised up, first in Spain, then in Austria, Russia, and finally in Germany an irrepressible opposition.

CONSULATE

Napoleon Bonaparte, First Consul of France (1800-1804). The Constitution of the Year VIII (1800) provided for three consuls and a tribunate and legislative body designated by the Senate from the general election lists. The First Consul conducted the administrative and foreign policies, had charge of the army, and proposed all laws. The real power, therefore, was concentrated in the First Consul, Napoleon Bonaparte.

Napoleon's Foreign Successes (1800-1804). Napoleon immediately turned his attention to the foreign problem of the Second Coalition. By intrigue, Napoleon got Russia not only to withdraw but also to revive an Armed Neutrality against Great Britain. Napoleon's victory at Marengo in Italy and Moreau's at Hohenlinden in Germany forced Austria to sue for peace. The Treaty of Lunéville (1801) strengthened that of Campo Formio. Although Great Britain had won the Battle of the Nile (1798) and had broken up the Armed Neutrality (1801), yet she could not conquer France, so she signed the Treaty of Amiens (1802), which was really only a truce. The Batavian, Helvetic, Ligurian, and Cisalpine republics in Holland, Switzerland, and Italy respectively were reëstablished. France was contented.

Permanent Internal Reforms of Napoleon. With the foreign problems temporarily settled, Napoleon turned his attention to internal reforms. The reforms under the Consulate are the most permanent of all Napoleon's contributions.

EQUALITY UNDER NAPOLEON. Bonaparte guaranteed equal justice, equal rights, equal opportunity, and the continued abolition of privilege—"careers open to talent." It was in the political sphere alone that Napoleon denied liberty.

CENTRALIZATION OF FRANCE. The government was completely centralized with its divisions of departments, arrondissements, and prefects making its officials directly responsible to the central government at Paris. All Napoleon's reforms reveal this centralizing tendency.

FINANCIAL STABILITY. In financial matters Napoleon was exacting in the collection of revenue and through rigid economy and by making the conquered of other lands support his army, he reduced the public expenditures. In 1800 he established the Bank of France.

CONCORDAT OF 1801. The ecclesiastical trouble was settled by the Concordat of 1801, by which the Pope concurred in the confiscation of Church property and in the assumption by the state of the power to nominate bishops who were in turn to appoint the priests. Napoleon agreed to have the State pay the clergy and the Pope was to invest the bishops with their office. Thus Church and State were welded closer together. By giving up the State's pretentions to spiritual leadership, Napoleon secured all he required in the way of temporal control. He ended one of the chief sources of opposition against himself, quieted the dissatisfaction of the peasants and others devoted to the old religion, and at the same time made it impossible for the Catholic hierarchy to exercise independent political power. This agreement regulated the Church and State until 1905.

CODE NAPOLÉON. The work of the National Convention in modifying the law was carried on by Napoleon. The Code Napoléon was composed of a civil code, a code of civil and criminal procedure, and a penal and commercial code. It was based upon the principle of equality. The Code Napoléon not only became the basic law of France, but it was carried to many of the countries conquered by France during the Napoleonic Wars, and thus became one of the important forces tending to break down the Old Régime outside France.

SYSTEM OF EDUCATION. The educational system of France was reorganized and centralized. The elementary schools were to be maintained by the commune under supervision of prefects or sub-prefects; the secondary schools were to be subject to governmental control, whether supported by public or private funds; lycées for higher learning were to be opened in every important town; and the University of France was to maintain uniformity throughout the system. Normal schools for the training of teachers were established. The whole movement gradually undermined the Catholic Church's previous monopoly of education.

PUBLIC WORKS. Many internal improvements were consummated at this time. Military roads emanating from Paris were constructed. Waterways were improved, canals dug, and bridges constructed. Paris was beautified.

PLEBISCITES OF 1802 AND 1804. The policy of Napoleon at home and on the continent increased his popularity among the majority. All open opposition was crushed out by the First Consul. The Jacobins and Royalists were obliged to attempt reform by secret intrigue. In 1802 Bonaparte had the Consulate

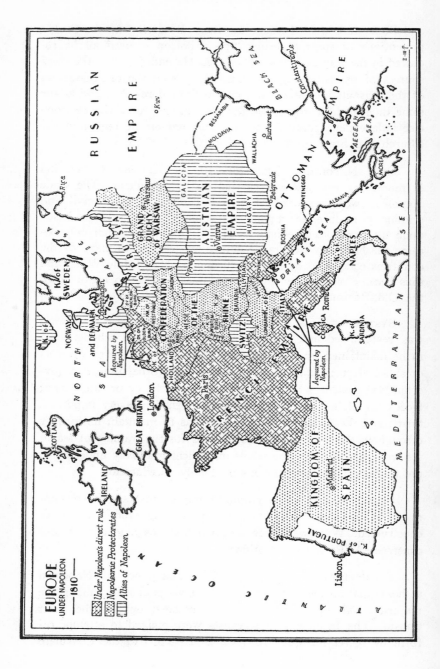

EUROPE
UNDER NAPOLEON
—— 1810 ——

Under Napoleon's direct rule
Napoleonic Protectorates
Allies of Napoleon

ATLANTIC OCEAN

K. of PORTUGAL

Lisbon

KINGDOM OF
SPAIN

Madrid

FRENCH EMPIRE

Paris

GREAT BRITAIN

London

SCOTLAND

IRELAND

NORTH SEA

K. of
NORWAY

K. of
SWEDEN

and DENMARK

Copenhagen

Riga

BALTIC SEA

PRUSSIA

RUSSIAN
EMPIRE

Kiev

GRAND
DUCHY
OF WARSAW

Warsaw

GALICIA

AUSTRIAN
EMPIRE

Vienna

Prague

HUNGARY

CONFEDERATION
OF THE
RHINE

BAVARIA

SWITZ.

HOLLAND

Acquired by
Napoleon

MECKL.
KM. OF
WESTPHALIA
HESSE
SAXONY

Acquired by
Napoleon

CORSICA
Rome
K. OF
SARDINIA

K. OF
NAPLES

MEDITERRANEAN SEA

ILLYRIAN
PROVINCES

ADRIATIC SEA

BOSNIA

Belgrade

MONTENEGRO

ALBANIA

OTTOMAN
EMPIRE

WALLACHIA

MOLDAVIA

BESSARABIA

Bucharest

BLACK SEA

Constantinople

OTTOMAN
EMPIRE

AEGEAN SEA

MOREA

114

bestowed upon himself for life by the plebiscite, and in 1804 another plebiscite made him a hereditary ruler—Emperor of the French.

FRENCH EMPIRE UNDER NAPOLEON
(1804-1814)

Napoleon as Emperor. As Emperor, Napoleon introduced a series of reforms which did away with some of the old republican customs, but the tricolor and much of the emotional significance of "Liberty, Equality, and Fraternity" were retained. With the smaller countries adjacent to France, Napoleon dealt in the most high-handed fashion. The Batavian Republic became the Kingdom of Holland with one of Napoleon's brothers as ruler. The Kingdom of Westphalia was created by Napoleon for his brother Jerome. A third brother was given the Kingdom of the Two Sicilies. All adverse criticism of Napoleon's absolutism was stifled by a vigorous censorship of the press.

Foreign Successes of Napoleon. The period of the Empire was one of continuous warfare through which the revolutionary seeds of France were scattered over the whole of Europe.

THIRD COALITION (1805). The Truce of Amiens (1802) came to an end the next year. Napoleon's continued interference in Italy, a rumor that he intended again to occupy Egypt, and a dispute over the surrender of Malta which Great Britain refused to give up as agreed at Amiens, precipitated the renewal of war. Napoleon seized Hanover and levied heavy contributions of men and material in preparation for the conflict. He established a great military camp at Boulogne and threatened England with invasion. Through the efforts of her Prime Minister, William Pitt the Younger, Great Britain induced Austria, Russia, and Sweden to join her in a third coalition against France.

TRAFALGAR (1805). The French and British navies came into conflict at Trafalgar. The combined Spanish and French fleets were completely defeated by Lord Nelson, and the continued supremacy of Great Britain on the seas was assured. Napoleon was forced by the ruin of his navy at Trafalgar to give up his ambitious scheme for an invasion of England. Throughout his subsequent career the invulnerability of England on the sea was the principal thorn in his side.

ULM AND AUSTERLITZ (1805). On land it was different. The Austrians were completely beaten at Ulm (October 21, 1805) and Vienna was taken. In December Napoleon defeated the Austrians and Russians under Francis II and Alexander I at Austerlitz. As a result of these battles Austria signed the Treaty of Pressburg (December, 1805) which reduced her to a second-rate power and increased Napoleon's strength and prestige. He was now able to rearrange the affairs of the minor German states to suit himself. He set up a new organization, the Confederation of the Rhine, with himself as protector. With the formation of the Confederation of the Rhine, the old Holy Roman Empire came to an end.

JENA (1806). Prussia joined the Third Coalition and declared war on France because of Napoleon's aggrandizement in Germany. But Prussia's help was shortlived, for the Duke of Brunswick was no match for the forces of Napoleon at the battle of Jena, and Napoleon entered Berlin in triumph.

FRIEDLAND (1807) AND PEACE OF TILSIT (1807). The Russians received a simliar humiliation at Friedland when Napoleon completely defeated them. Alexander readily accepted Napoleon's offer for peace. Together they arranged the Peace of Tilsit, which did not exact any Russian soil, but which reduced Prussia to a third-rate power by disarming her, taking nearly half her possessions, and demanding a heavy indemnity. The peace destroyed the Third Coalition.

SUBJECTION OF SWEDEN. With the help of Denmark and Russia, Napoleon was able to bring Sweden to terms. Russia took Finland and the Aaland Islands. Upon request, the Swedish King, Gustavus IV, was forced to abdicate in favor of his uncle, Charles XIII (1809-1818), who promised to name one of Napoleon's marshalls, General Bernadotte, as heir. Thus Napoloen would be able to control Sweden.

NAPOLEON AS MASTER OF EUROPE (1808). Napoleon reached his greatest heights in 1808, when he had practically the whole of Europe, with the exception of England, under his sway. He cut up the map to his own satisfaction. In the Germanies Napoleon reduced the number of states from over three hundred to less than one hundred. He did away with the Holy Roman Empire (1806), and Francis II, the last Holy Roman Emperor, became Emperor of Austria. The Confederation of the Rhine (1806) was organized, consisting of many of the states of the old Empire. Over all his conquered territories he abolished feudalism and serfdom, recognized equality of all citizens, and instituted the Code Napoléon. Even though he had curbed liberty, yet equality and fraternity had widened their scope to such an extent that their effects in Europe could never be eradicated.

DECLINE OF NAPOLEON'S POWER

Causes for Downfall of French Empire. The causes for the Empire's downfall are apparent. In the first place, the success of this venture depended entirely upon one man—Napoleon—and the legend of invincibility that grew up about him. Secondly, the Empire had been built upon a military basis. The old enthusiasm gave out and conscripted forces were not keen believers in the "destiny" of Liberty, Equality, and Fraternity. Thirdly, Napoleon's method of quartering his soldiers in foreign countries served to arouse the people against France and the revolution and to increase a nationalistic feeling against them. Finally, there was the persistent opposition of England, secure because of her insular position and her sea power. Most of Napoleon's later wars were undertaken to strike indirectly at Great Britain. It was Great Britain that tirelessly stirred up and subsidized new coalitions and rebellions.

Continental System. The war between Great Britain and France is characterized by the "Continental System," by which Napoleon attacked the commerce and industry of Great Britain by preventing the importation of English goods to the continent. The Berlin and Milan Decrees (1806-1807) placed a paper blockade on England. Great Britain retaliated with the British Orders in Council (1807) which declared that only British ships could trade with France and her allies. Neutral ships were bound to suffer. With a large navy, the British were better able to enforce their orders than was Napoleon, his decrees. The enforcing of the Continental System proved a gigantic task, and it aroused opposition in Italy, Holland, Portugal, Spain, and Russia.

NAPOLEON AND POPE PIUS VII. When the Pope, Pius VII, refused to enforce Napoleon's decrees in the papal states and dared to excommunicate Napoleon, the former was taken prisoner and deprived of his temporal power, while Napoleon incorporated the papal states into the French Empire.

DETHRONEMENT OF LOUIS NAPOLEON. In Holland Louis Napoleon was dethroned because he admitted English goods. Napoleon annexed that country to France.

NAPOLEON AND PORTUGAL. The favorable commercial relations between England and Portugal, which dated back to the Treaty of Methuen (1703), needed to be broken for the success of Napoleon's system. After Tilsit Portugal was commanded to adhere to the decrees. Upon her refusal Napoleon dispatched his forces for Portugal, and with Spanish permission they crossed the peninsula, entered Lisbon (October, 1807), and declared the Continental System in force. The Portuguese royal family fled to Brazil.

Rise of National Opposition.

NAPOLEON AND SPAIN. The weak Bourbon rulers of Spain were no match for the intrigues of Napoleon, and they gave up the throne. Napoleon made his brother, Joseph Bonaparte, King of Spain (1808). Joseph Bonaparte proceeded to give Spain the liberal reforms of the revolution and to enforce strictly the Continental System. However, the Spanish objected to having a "foreign king" and rose up against Joseph, forcing him and his French troops to flee from Madrid. Great Britain promised to send aid not only to the Iberian peninsula but to any other country that rose up against "the common enemy of all nations." The Duke of Wellington subsequently landed in Portugal (August, 1808) with a British army, and the great Peninsular War was under way (1808-1813). The unexpected national resistance of the Spanish people, the difficulties of the terraine, and the skill of the British commanders ultimately defeated the French. The

Spanish adventure cost Napoleon hundreds of thousands of troops. It was the first time he had directly encountered the new force of national patriotism that was ultimately to destroy him.

NAPOLEON AND AUSTRIA. Austria, smarting under the humiliating defeats by Napoleon in 1805-1806, had been preparing for a conflict with the French Emperor by instituting military reform and instilling a feeling of patriotism among the people. That country's declaration of war came when Napoleon was occupied in Spain, but his immediate quelling of that disturbance left him free to turn to the Archduke Charles and his Austrians. The victory of the Austrians at Aspern (May, 1809) was not followed up, and Napoleon rallied his forces and crushingly defeated the Austrians at Wagram (July, 1809). At this time Francis I accepted the Treaty of Vienna (1809) by which he gave up Western Galicia to Warsaw, Eastern Galicia to Russia, the Illyrian provinces to France, and Tyrol to Bavaria. To insure Austria's support of France, Napoleon set his wife, Josephine, aside and married Maria Louisa, daughter of Francis I of Austria. But the forced friendship between France and Austria was hollow. In this war, as in Spain, the new element of national resistance was evident.

NAPOLEON AND PRUSSIA. Prussia, smarting under the defeat at Jena, instituted a system of reform through which many of the "old régime" conditions were cast aside. Under Baron von Stein and Chancellor Hardenberg serfdom was done away with, local self-government was extended, many restrictions on trade and industry were removed, and universal compulsory military service was put into force. A common school system was laid out by Wilhelm von Humboldt and the University of Berlin established (1809). It was in Prussia that the new spirit of national patriotism showed its greatest strength. There was a tremendous growth of patriotic activity and a great deepening of national consciousness. In 1813 this spirit flamed up, much as French patriotism had flamed up in 1792-1795, and the whole nation rushed to arms with wild enthusiasm.

NAPOLEON AND RUSSIA. Trouble with Russia had been brewing since 1809. The disastrous effects of the continental system were too great, and Alexander I gradually abandoned its enforcement. This meant war with Napoleon. With an army of 600,000 men made up of French, Germans, Italian, Poles, and others, Napoleon was ready in April, 1812, to challenge the 400,000 Russians under General Kutusov. Napoleon was allowed to cross the Niemen and advance beyond, pursuing the ever retreating Russians. Napoleon pushed on, until he finally gained possession of Moscow, but its destruction by fire made it impossible for Napoleon to winter his army of 100,000 in the city because of the lack of supplies, so he withdrew. With the severe winter taking its toll of starved and frozen, and with the Russians constantly attacking and killing the men, the Grande Armée was less than 50,000 strong when it recrossed the Niemen in December and took refuge in Germany. The invasion of Russia had cost Napoleon nearly half a million soldiers. The loss proved fatal.

"WAR OF LIBERATION" (1813).   Through the efforts of Prussia, Russia was induced to refrain from signing a treaty with Napoleon and to join a coalition composed of Prussia, Great Britain, and Sweden for the purpose of breaking up Napoleon's power. Once Russia had joined the coalition, Frederick William declared war on Napoleon (1813), and the War of Liberation was under way. Napoleon quickly organized a new army and defeated the Russians and Prussians in battles at Lutzen and Bautzen. An armistice merely resulted in a further concentration of forces by Napoleon and the members of the coalition, who were now joined by Austria. The climax came in the Battle of Leipzig ("Battle of the Nations" October, 1813), in which Napoleon could not stand the onslaught of the Allies, and after losing 40,000 men and 30,000 prisoners he retreated, crossed the Rhine, and left Germany free. The French Empire collapsed, and only Polish Warsaw and Saxony remained loyal. Napoleon was not ready to throw up the game, however, and he began organizing a new army for a final attempt at victory. He refused the offer of the Allies which would have left him supreme in a France bounded by the Alps, the Rhine, and the Pyrenees.

ABDICATION OF NAPOLEON (1814).   The campaign of 1814 in France found Napoleon trying to keep the Russians, Austrians, and Prussians out of northern France. The British under Wellington, who had driven the French from Spain, were coming from the south, and another Austrian army was returning from Lombardy and Venetia to threaten France. Napoleon was no match for such overwhelming odds, and Paris finally surrendered to the Allies in March, 1814. Napoleon abdicated and accepted the sovereignty of the island of Elba in the Mediterranean, where he spent the next ten months.

PRELIMINARY CONGRESS OF VIENNA (1814). While Napoleon was at Elba, the European monarchs set about to restore the old order under the new found principle of "legitimacy." The brother of Louis XVI was crowned Louis XVIII, and he restored the old régime as far as he dared, but he did not insist on absolute monarchy. He accepted the limitations imposed upon him by the events of the Revolution. Ferdinand VII was restored to the throne of Spain, and Pope Pius VII returned to Rome (he had been virtually a prisoner of Napoleon since 1809). A congress met at Vienna to settle the problems caused by the downfall of Napoleon.

ONE HUNDRED DAYS (1815). Napoleon, while at Elba, saw that the European countries were so taken up with other matters that it would be difficult for them quickly to ally themselves together against him, and he felt that the French would welcome his return. Succeeding in effecting his escape from the island, he returned to France and was accepted by the people and the army. Without firing a shot, he entered the capital (March, 1815) and promised to save France from the outrages of the returning nobles, and to renounce war and conquest. The four great powers Great Britain, Prussia, Austria, and Russia forgot their own jealousies and once more joined together to rid Europe permanently of Napoleon. They organized a great army with divisions under Wellington, Blücher, and Schwarzenberg and proceeded toward France. Napoleon started for the border intent on meeting each singly and defeating them, but at Waterloo (June 18, 1815) he was defeated by the Duke of Wellington assisted by the timely arrival on the battlefield of 65,000 Prussians under Blücher.

NAPOLEON BANISHED TO ST. HELENA. Napoleon returned to Paris and abdicated in favor of his son, but the French Parliament, under Lafayette, set up a provisional government and Louis XVIII was once more restored. Napoleon gave himself up to the British and was sent to the Island of St. Helena, where he spent the last five and a half years of his life writing his memoirs and meditating over the past.

Significance of Napoleonic Age.   The effects of the Napoleonic Era are to be found in all phases of activity—social, political, cultural, religious, and economic.

LIBERTÉ, ÉGALITÉ, AND FRATERNITÉ FROM 1804-1815.   The period gave a new meaning to the watchwords of the revolution— Liberty, Equality, and Fraternity.

Liberty found expression in the popular sovereignty of the Consulate and the Empire. Although the right of private property, of freedom of conscience and of worship were granted, yet speech and the press were severely censored.

Equality was intended for all that came under Napoleon's sway. Feudalism and serfdom were abolished, and the social equalities contained in the Code Napoléon were guaranteed.

Fraternity received its greatest impetus at this time. National patriotism was extended throughout all Europe. Thus the total effect of the Napoleonic period was to confirm and consolidate the French Revolution and so stamp its ideas on Europe that they have never been eradicated. Thoroughly contemptuous himself of the idealism and altruistic passion of the Revolution and interested only in his own aggrandizement, Napoleon was nevertheless the accidental agent that made for the ultimate triumph of the Revolution.

REMAKING MAP OF EUROPE.   Politically this period caused a remaking of the map of Europe at Vienna. Great Britain set about to appropriate many of the French colonies and some of the Dutch. Great Britain's commerce was greatly increased by the unsettled conditions in Spain which led her colonies to open their ports to England's shipping. To foster this commerce Great Britain had the benefits of the great Industrial Revolution, which had not yet reached the continent because of the European conflicts.

(See page 137 for Congress of Vienna.)

CHAPTER XVI.

THE INDUSTRIAL REVOLUTION

The Industrial Revolution, a movement the early phases of which took place in England between 1770 and 1825 and in continental Europe after 1815, changed fundamentally the industrial, commercial, political, and social life of the Western World. It consisted mainly in the application of machinery to manufacturing, mining, transportation, communication, and agriculture, and in the changes in economic organization that attended these innovations of methods. The large scale and basic nature of the changes introduced in a period of about sixty years justifies the term "revolution," although the scientific and economic background extends for centuries into the past, and the movement is still going forward at a rate perhaps greater today than ever before.

BACKGROUND OF INDUSTRIAL REVOLUTION

Agriculture. In the middle of the eighteenth century the customs of economic life were little different from those of the Middle Ages. In agriculture the inefficient "open-field" system prevailed. Each peasant cultivated a number of small separated strips of land, into which the large arable fields were divided, and grazed his livestock on the "common" or uncultivated pasture that was free to all. Fertilization of soil, rotation of crops, and controlled breeding of livestock were unknown. One third of the cultivated land lay fallow every year. Crop yields were poor. The communal organization made innovations of method difficult.

Manufacturing. Etymologically the word "manufacture" means "make by hand." Handicraft was the only method of production. Because it supplied a basic human need, the textile industry dwarfed all others in importance. The making of thread from raw wool and later from cotton (spinning) and the making of cloth from thread (weaving) were the two chief processes of textile manufacture. In the eighteenth century the industry was carried on chiefly in the home with simple hand tools (spinning wheel, hand-loom) requiring little outlay of money. Under this "domestic" system each family was supplied with raw material by a middleman known as a "factor," who also purchased the finished product. Most families carried on a variety of industries—farming in the spring and summer, clothmaking in the winter. Production of goods was essentially production for use, not production for profit in a free market, since the market was small and local, and the amount of goods it would absorb was definitely known in advance.

General Economic and Social Conditions. Travel and transportation were difficult and slow. Stagecoaches, sailing vessels, and river barges were the chief means. Little money was in circulation. The rigid class stratification of society and the illiteracy of the mass of the population prevented most men from improving their condition by thrift and enterprise. Government was monarchial (continental Europe) or oligarchic (Great Britain).

CAUSES OF
THE INDUSTRIAL REVOLUTION

Commercial Expansion. The explorations and colonial establishments of the sixteenth and seventeenth centuries led to a great expansion of commerce, to the increased use of a money exchange system, and to the growth of a strong class of business men and capitalists. While the effect of this commercial revolution on technology was not immediate, the enlargement of the economic horizon showed shrewd men unlimited opportunities for money-making if production could be increased. The commercial expansion opened up a world market ripe for exploitation, made available an abundant supply of raw materials, and implanted a new psychology of enterprise.

Scientific Progress. For two centuries there had been steady accumulation of scientific knowledge although little practical use had been made of it. But the researches in pure science of such men as Galileo, Newton, Huygens, and Boyle laid the foundations on which later practical experimenters were able to build.

Favorable Political Organization. A necessary condition for the coming of the Industrial Revolution was the establishment of a considerable degree of political freedom, and the break-up of the medieval gild system in industry and of the feudal system of land tenure. This was accomplished in England by the revolutions of the seventeenth century, and in continental Europe by the French Revolution and the changes spread abroad by the Napoleonic conquests.

Readiness of England to Take Lead. Conditions in England were particularly favorable for the beginning of the Industrial Revolution. England had achieved a higher degree of national unity and political stability than other European countries. Though much less populous than France, England had become, through her successful wars in the eighteenth century, the leading maritime and colonial power of the world. She had also advanced further than other nations in the organization of capitalism; she had a strong banking system and an abundance of capital seeking profitable investment. England's natural resources, notably an abundance of coal and iron ore, enabled her to outdistance her rivals, particularly after the introduction of iron smelting by coal instead of charcoal (c. 1750), and the widespread use of steam power (after 1785). The humid climate of England was ideal for cotton spinning. Finally, the disorder on the continent attending the French Revolution and the Napoleonic Wars delayed the acceptance of the Industrial Revolution in France, Germany, and the Low Countries.

Revolution in Agriculture. In the eighteenth century many innovations in agricultural methods and organization brought far-reaching changes that foreshadowed and promoted the Industrial Revolution. Jethro Tull (1674-1741) introduced the machine "drill" which displaced the wasteful method of broadcast seed-sowing. He also pioneered in the use of artificial fertilization. Charles Viscount ("Turnip") Townshend (1674-1738) made experiments with crop rotation. Robert Bakewell (1725-1795) showed that the quality of live stock could be improved by selective breeding. In England, in the late eighteenth century, a large amount of farm land and common was "enclosed"—taken over and consolidated with large estates—sometimes with compensation to the small peasants who had previously cultivated it, often without any compensation. The enclosure movement greatly improved agricultural efficiency and the total crop yield of land, but deprived large numbers of small peasants of their livelihoods and forced them to migrate to the cities in search of employment.

INVENTIONS OF
THE INDUSTRIAL REVOLUTION

Textile Industry. A small improvement introduced by John Kay (1733) led to a series of inventions. Kay's "flying shuttle" speeded up the process of weaving and thus increased the demand for thread. James Hargreaves' "spinning jenny" (1767), followed by Richard Arkwright's "water frame" (a water-power operated spinning machine (1769), and Samuel Crompton's "spinning mule" (1779) supplied the demand for thread and created a surplus. Edmund Cartwright's "power loom" (1785) improved weaving methods and thus restored the balance between spinning and weaving. Eli Whitney's "cotton gin" (United States, 1793) made available a large cheap supply of raw cotton for spinning. The net effect of these inventions was to multiply many times the amount of cloth that could be made by a given group of workers.

Steam Power. Fundamental in the new industrial order was the development of a cheap, portable source of power. James Watt's invention of the condenser (1769) and of a practical method of converting the reciprocating motion of the piston into rotary motion (1781) made the steam engine (crude forms of which had been invented earlier by Papin and Newcomen) a practical prime mover for all kinds of machinery. The steam engine soon largely displaced water wheels and windmills. It facilitated and made necessary the production of great quantities of coal and iron. Applications of the steam engine were rapidly discovered. On water Robert Fulton's steamboat, the *Clermont* (1807), and on land George Stephenson's rail locomotive (1825) were the forerunners of modern transportation. The steam printing press (1814) decreased the cost of printed matter and facilitated the spread of universal education.

Coal, Iron, and Steel. Early in the eighteenth century Abraham Darby and his son made experiments in the substitution of coke (made from coal) for charcoal (from wood) for the reduction of iron ore. In 1760 John Smeaton improved the Darby process by the addition of a water-power driven air blast that improved the quality and yield of coke. About 1784 Henry Cort introduced the "puddling" process for the purification of pig iron made with coke. From this time forward coal and iron went hand in hand with steam as the foundation of industrialization. Later developments of prime importance were the invention (1859) of the "Bessemer process" and of the "open-hearth process" for the large scale manufacture of steel.

Communications. With the development of railways and steam navigation, travel and communication became much more rapid. A penny postal system was introduced in Great Britain in 1840. But the greatest improvement was the practically instantaneous communication by electricity introduced with Morse's telegraph (1837). The development of electrical science late in the nineteenth century led to the invention of Bell's telephone (1876) and Marconi's wireless (1896).

Farming Machinery. The application of machines to farming revolutionized agriculture. A threshing machine driven by steam was used in England as early as 1803. Later came McCormick's reaper (1834) and steam-driven plows and cultivators (c. 1850).

Machine Manufacture of Machinery. The early textile machines were made of wood and hand-worked iron. One of the important results of the introduction of steam power and large scale iron-making was the application of machinery to the manufacture of machinery. The lathe, the grinder, and the milling cutter for working metals made machines the breeders of more machines and help to explain how the Industrial Revolution expanded with great rapidity after a start had been made. Standardization of parts, which is fundamental in all mass production, was made both necessary and easy by the use of machinery.

Invention after 1830. The early advance of the Industrial Revolution, while rapid compared with previous technological progress, was utterly dwarfed by the flood of invention that came in an ever-increasing tide after 1830. Among hundreds of machines, processes, and scientific principles may be mentioned (1) Faraday's discovery of electromagnetic induction (1831), (2) large scale preservation of food by canning (c. 1845), (3) Daguerre's invention of photography (1839), (4) Ericsson's screw propeller (1836), and (5) Goodyear's rubber vulcanization (1844).

So great was the acceleration of invention in the nineteenth century that some historians speak of a "Second Industrial Revolution," beginning about 1870 and including the enormous development of electrical technology and of industries dependent on internal combustion engines that occurred during the following forty years.

ECONOMIC RESULTS OF
THE INDUSTRIAL REVOLUTION

The Factory System. The old method of small production in the home with one's own tools could not meet the competition of machine production, and the cost of machinery was prohibitive to the individual workers. Hence arose the factory system, i.e., large scale production in factories using machines owned by the employer. The factory system stimulated the growth of *division of labor* and of *mass production* through standardization of processes and parts.

Expansion of Industry and Increase of Wealth. Old industries began to produce on a much larger scale than previously. New industries sprang up offering new goods to satisfy man's desires. Particularly significant was the rise of the *producers' goods* industry as distinguished from the *consumers' goods* industry. The increasing productiveness of the machines led to an enormous total increase in wealth, but the surplus was at first concentrated in the hands of a comparatively few rich men. In the long run the total increase in wealth led to a general rise in standards of living.

Rise of Industrial Capitalism. The controllers of the newly created surplus wealth were the industrial capitalists who owned the factories. As the Industrial Revolution proceeded, the power and influence of the industrial capitalists grew ever greater, and it was they who shaped the course of further industrialization by reinvesting their gains in new enterprises rather than distributing the increase to the general population. So great was the productiveness of the machines that in spite of lavish personal expenditures on non-productive display, only a relatively small fraction of the total increase in wealth was immediately consumed. The rapid development (after 1830) of the limited-liability joint-stock corporation greatly facilitated the investment of surplus capital and led to rapid promotion of new industry.

Economic Imperialism. The great problem of the capitalists was the profitable investment of their wealth. The development of multiplied productivity required an ever larger market for the disposal of the product. Hence arose, especially in the later nineteenth century when domestic markets had begun to reach a saturation point, the pressure for imperialistic expansion and "spheres of influence" in the undeveloped parts of the world.

Booms and Depressions. As production for profit in a free market replaced production for use, and as innovations of method upset the balance in established industries, the phenomena of large scale "booms" and "depressions" introduced a new element into economic life.

International Economic Dependence. The Industrial Revolution enormously accelerated the movement toward international economic dependence that had begun with the Commercial Revolution of the sixteenth and seventeenth centuries. The cotton spindles of England, to take a single instance, depended upon a steady supply of raw cotton from the slave-worked plantations of the United States. As the population of Europe, especially of England, became more and more engaged in urban industry, they raised less food on their farms and became heavy importers of wheat, meat, and tropical food products. In exchange for food, Europe exported manufactured goods. The entire world became a market place. Dislocation of industry in any part of the world often has important repercussions in countries thousands of miles away.

SOCIAL RESULTS OF
THE INDUSTRIAL REVOLUTION

Dependent Proletariat Concentrated in Cities. With the rise of the factory system came a shifting of population from small agricultural villages to the cities. A vast urban proletariat grew up, propertyless, largely illiterate, and entirely dependent upon wage earning for a living.

Bad Labor and Living Conditions. The rapid growth of the industrial cities that paid no attention to sanitation or comfort produced foul slums where the masses lived in horrible squalor. With no concern for the welfare of the wage-earner the capitalist and his agents offered small wages in return for long hours in unhealthful factories.

Large Scale Child Labor. Because little strength or training was required to tend the machines, women and particularly children ranging in ages from six years up were employed in large numbers and mercilessly exploited. Children of pauper parents were farmed out to factory owners on terms that amounted to slavery, unprotected even by the "property interest" that mitigated the rigors of true slavery, and were literally worked to death. These hideous conditions lasted for more than half a century in England but were gradually bettered through the agitation of reformers and the quickening of public conscience.

Insecurity and Mass Unemployment. Because the supply of labor, considered as a commodity, was usually in excess of the demand, and because the workers were without any independent means of subsistence, the fear of loss of the job became a constant specter in the worker's mind. Besides the possibility of discharge for some delinquency there was the danger of large scale shut-downs as a consequence of business depressions. Mass unemployment, new in modern history, became one of the gravest social problems arising from the Industrial Revolution.

Mechanization of Warfare. A far-reaching consequence of the Industrial Revolution was the development of highly efficient mechanized weapons that rendered war immensely more destructive and dangerous to civilized progress.

POLITICAL RESULTS OF THE INDUSTRIAL REVOLUTION

Strengthening of the Bourgeoisie (Middle Class.) In England the bourgeoisie attained a large measure of political power through the Reform Bill of 1832, which redistributed seats in Parliament to grant representation to the new industrial centers and to diminish the representation of the so-called "rotten boroughs;" and which gave the right to vote to a large new group of the moderately well-to-do (*ten pound tenants*). It was bourgeoisie sentiment, made politically articulate by the Reform Bill and led by such able men as Richard Cobden, John Bright, and Charles Villiers that brought about the repeal (1846, following a terrible famine in Ireland) of the Corn Laws, that had long subsidized the land-owning aristocracy at the expense of the rest of the people. The bourgeoisie were also successful in putting down the agitation of the Chartists, which was essentially an effort to secure for the lower classes the same political powers as had been obtained by the bourgeoisie through the Reform Bill.

In France the position of the bourgeoisie was strengthened by the Revolution of 1830, which put Louis Philippe on the throne as a constitutional king and provided for effective control of the government by the middle class as in England.

The formation of the *Zollverein,* or Customs Union, in Germany (1834) established a protective tariff, which benefitted the bourgeoisie. This offered an example of unification for commercial purposes that was later to foster the political consolidation of Germany.

Rise of Labor as a Political Force. The new proletariat created by the Industrial Revolution, though hampered by poverty, ignorance, and lack of leadership, gradually developed a feeling of common consciousness and sought means to improve their condition by political agitation, combination in Trade Unions, and various types of coöperative action. With the advance of democracy, which was partly favored by the bourgeoisie, the laboring classes grew stronger politically and were finally able to make their influence felt directly in elections and plebiscites. Nevertheless, the slowness of the improvement in the economic condition of the working class and the bitter opposition toward the rise of labor on the part of conservatives in the upper and middle classes gave rise to radical movements among the workers, based on a belief that no reform short of overthrow of the existing capitalistic system could be of much benefit in the long run.

Dependence of Military Superiority on Industrialization. The Industrial Revolution led to a new balance of world powers as it became ever more clear that military strength depended on industrialization. The thoroughness of the Industrial Revolution in England, France, and Germany, and its relative weakness in Russia and Eastern Europe, generally was the most powerful factor contributing to the European dominance by the first three states at the beginning of the twentieth century. The Europeanizing of the world in the nineteenth century carried the Industrial Revolution with it: so Japan, by its sudden acceptance of the Industrial Revolution in the later nineteenth century, became the dominant power of the Orient: so the industrialized Northern United States were able to defeat the South in the American Civil War.

INTELLECTUAL AND CULTURAL RESULTS OF THE INDUSTRIAL REVOLUTION

Adam Smith and Laissez Faire. The social and economic changes made by the Industrial Revolution stimulated the growth of the science of economics or "political economy" as it was usually called. Nineteenth century economic thinking stems chiefly from Adam Smith, whose *Wealth of Nations* (1776) argued forcibly for non-interference by government with business. Smith held that each man is the best judge of his own economic affairs; that the free play of competition and the universal desire for enrichment would result in the maximum increase in total wealth; and that though individuals might be selfish and unconcerned with the common good, their collective activity would automatically, as if guided by an "invisible hand," tend to the economic welfare of all. Smith thus powerfully supported the economic doctrine known in France as laissez faire; government should be merely an omnipresent policeman protecting property and compelling the performance of contracts. This laissez faire doctrine appealed strongly to the new capitalists of the Industrial Revolution.

The Classical Economists. The ideas of Smith were developed and elaborated by the school of "classical economists," the leaders of which were Thomas Malthus, David Ricardo, Nassau Senior, and James Mill. In 1798 Malthus formulated his "principle of population," which asserted that any improvement in the economic condition of the poor would be counterbalanced by an increase in population, since population tends to increase to the limit of the means of subsistence. It therefore followed that grinding poverty and a high death rate from starvation, disease, and war must forever be the lot of the mass of mankind. The only conceivable alternative (which Malthus hardly took seriously) was the limitation of the population by "moral restraint." Ricardo enunciated the celebrated "iron law of wages," which stated that wages must inevitably tend to an amount just capable of maintaining life, much as the coal fed into a steam engine was just capable of maintaining the fire under the boiler.

The Socialists. Against the terrible, if cheerful, pessimism of the individualist economists arose the socialists, who refused to accept as irremediable the bad conditions brought by the Industrial Revolution. Robert Owen's experiment at New Lanark, Scotland, was a coöperative community scheme for improving the condition of the worker. The success of the New Lanark experiment raised hopes for a rapid amelioration of social conditions, but later experiments of the same sort by Owen and others were disappointing. In France, Saint-Simon, Fourier, and Louis Blanc tried to improve conditions, but their idealistic schemes were not practical. However, they created a public opinion against the system of laissez faire, which demanded and obtained better working conditions, a higher standard of living, an increased leisure, and a greater freedom for women and children.

Rise of Engineering and Research. The Industrial Revolution immensely stimulated scientific investigation. As manufacturing techniques became more complex, experts were required to manage and improve them. The profession of engineering became indispensable to the industrial civilization. Science began to be more and more pursued for its services to technology. In time, large scale industrial endowment of laboratory research became the accepted way of forwarding invention. The achievements of the new applied science appealed powerfully to the imagination of the common man.

Secularization of Interests. The progress of the Industrial Revolution eventually placed an undreamed-of variety of material goods in the hands of a large part of the population. The mass-circulation newspaper, the automobile, the motion picture and the radio—all products of the Industrial Revolution—have supplied man with a whole new set of interests, and, far more than the arguments of philosophical agnosticism, have brought about the secularization of viewpoint and widespread religious indifferentism that is characteristic of contemporary life.

CHAPTER XVII.

METTERNICHISM

The downfall of Napoleon (1814-1815) resulted in a general resettlement of European affairs at the Congress of Vienna. The period 1815-1830 is often called the "Era of Metternich" because the policies and influence of Prince Clemens Metternich, Austrian Chancellor and Foreign Minister, were dominant in continental Europe, and because the main political and social movement of the times arose from the conflict between the supporters and the opponents of Metternich's ideas. Leading characteristics of Metternichism were (1) support of political absolutism, (2) suppression of nationalistic ambitions, and (3) forcible preservation of the *status quo* as established by the Congress of Vienna. Metternichism may thus be summed up as reaction from the French Revolution and the ideas it had spread abroad. Opposed to Metternichism was the movement known as "liberalism." Liberalism favored greater political, intellectual, and economic freedom for the individual. It also favored nationalistic aspirations. It found its support in two principal groups: (1) the intellectuals, patriots, and romantics who were inspired by the eighteenth century "enlightenment" and by the French Revolution with its doctrines of the "Rights of Man" and of "Liberty, Equality, and Fraternity," and (2) the rising moneyed class or bourgeoisie whom the

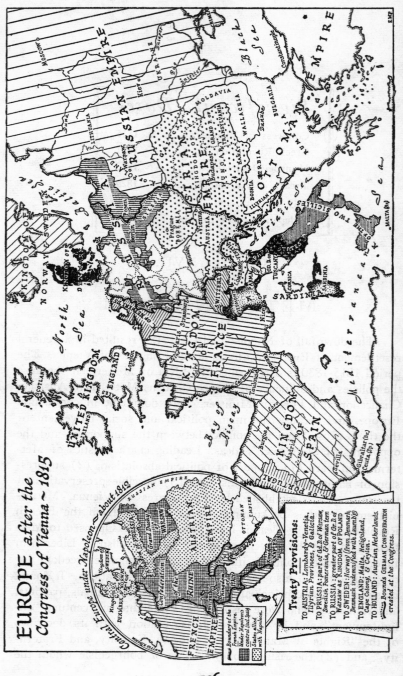

EUROPE after the
Congress of Vienna ~ 1815

Central Europe under Napoleon ~ about 1812

Treaty Provisions:

TO AUSTRIA: *Lombardy-Venetia, Illyrian Provinces, & Galicia.*
TO PRUSSIA: *part of Gd.D.of Warsaw, Swedish Pomerania, & German terr.*
TO RUSSIA: *greater part of Gr.D.of Warsaw as KINGDOM OF POLAND*
TO SWEDEN: *Norway (from Denmark, Denmark indemnified with Lauenbg)*
TO ENGLAND: *Malta, Heligoland, Cape Colony, & Ceylon.*
TO HOLLAND: *Austrian Netherlands.*
Bounds GERMAN CONFEDERATION created at the Congress.

RUSSIAN EMPIRE

KINGDOM OF NORWAY

KINGDOM OF DENMARK

KINGDOM OF SWEDEN

North Sea

UNITED KINGDOM

SCOTLAND

IRELAND

ENGLAND

London

Baltic Sea

POLAND

Kiev

UKRAINE

Moscow

AUSTRIAN EMPIRE

BOHEMIA
Prague

Vienna

KINGDOM OF HUNGARY
Budapest

TRANSYLVANIA

GALICIA

MOLDAVIA

WALLACHIA

SERBIA

BOSNIA

BULGARIA

Danube

OTTOMAN EMPIRE

RUMELIA

Constantinople

Black Sea

Aegean Sea

KINGDOM OF FRANCE
Paris

Bay of Biscay

KINGDOM OF SPAIN
Madrid

Burgos

Seville

PORTUGAL

Gibraltar (Br.)
Ceuta (Sp.)

Mediterranean Sea

SWITZ.

SARDINIA

THE TWO SICILIES

PAPAL STATES

TUSCANY

CORSICA

K. OF SARDINIA

Adriatic Sea

MALTA (Br.)

E.M.P.

Industrial Revolution was enriching and who desired political power to increase and consolidate their economic gains. A large part of nineteenth century history is concerned with the growth of this double-rooted liberal movement and its struggle with the forces of conservatism.

THE CONGRESS OF VIENNA

Leaders. Besides Prince Metternich, the important diplomats at Vienna were Talleyrand for France, Hardenberg and von Humboldt for Prussia, Nesselrode and Rasoumoffsky for Russia, and Castlereagh and Wellington for Great Britain. Tsar Alexander I of Russia, Emperor Francis I of Austria, and King Frederick William III of Prussia also attended in person. With the exception of Alexander I, a dreamy idealist easily manipulated by such a master of the diplomatic art as Metternich, all these men were devoted to the *ancien régime*.

"Legitimacy" and "Compensations." The watchwords of the Congress of Vienna were "Legitimacy" and "Compensations." By legitimacy was meant the principle that the dynastic changes introduced by Napoleon were to be undone and Europe restored to its "legitimate" rulers and their descendants as of 1792. The doctrine of legitimacy was a clever invention of the French diplomat Talleyrand, who wished to prevent any partitioning or other diminution of French territory. Legitimacy fell in well with the reactionary policies of Metternich. By pressing the doctrine of legitimacy and by skillfully taking advantage of quarrels among his opponents, Talleyrand was able to get much lighter terms for France than might have been expected from the magnitude of the Napoleonic Wars and the completeness of the French defeat. Even the temporary return of Napoleon (the Hundred Days) did not result in a very vindictive punishment. In the name of legitimacy the monarchs of France, Spain, Holland, and the Italian states were restored to their thrones. Carried to its logical conclusion, the doctrine of legitimacy would have also restored the territorial boundaries exactly as they were before the Revolution, but the Great Powers did not wish to do this. Each desired some of the spoils of victory. Accordingly, under the euphemistic term "compensations," Great Britain retained the French and Dutch colonies she had seized, Holland was compensated by being allowed to annex the Austrian Netherlands (present-day Belgium), Austria was compensated by receiving Venetia and Milan in Italy, while Hapsburg rulers were seated on the thrones of Tuscany, Modena, and Parma. The Germanies were reorganized into a loose confederation of thirty-eight states with Austria the outstanding member. Prussia received part of Saxony and some land along the Rhine. Sweden was given Norway in return for Finland, over which Russia had gained control in 1809. Outside the realm of "legitimacy" and "compensations," almost the only constructive reform of the Congress of Vienna was a pious gesture against the African Slave Trade.

Suppression of Nationalistic Ambitions. The total disregard by the Congress of Vienna of the principle of national self-determination made most of its work temporary and provided fuel for many revolutions in the nineteenth century.

Machinery for Enforcing the Vienna Settlement. Immediately after the Congress of Vienna, two alliance systems were formed to preserve the settlement. The first was the so-called Holy Alliance, proposed by the pious Alexander I, and joined by Russia, Austria, and Prussia. The Holy Alliance was intended by the Tsar to give expression in international affairs to the precepts of Christianity—justice, charity, and peace. The Holy Alliance was later joined by most of the other states of Europe. In the hands of the realistic diplomacy of Metternich and others, the Holy Alliance proved to be nothing but the "verbiage" that Metternich called it, but in the minds of the liberals of the time it became a symbol for everything reactionary and suppressive. It was not, however, the Holy Alliance but the Quadruple Alliance —an agreement of Austria, Great Britain, Prussia, and Russia— that actually furnished the teeth of the Vienna settlement. Although deserted a short time later by Great Britain, the Quadruple Alliance, with Metternich as its directing genius, dominated European affairs during most of the period 1815-1830. Under the Quadruple Alliance agreement, a series of international congresses was held (Aix-la-Chapelle, 1818; Troppau, 1820; Laibach, 1821; Verona, 1822), which took collective action to crush out liberalism wherever it might appear, even arranging for armed intervention in the internal affairs of friendly states.

TRIUMPH OF REACTION (1815-1830)

France Under Louis XVIII and Charles X. In 1815 Louis XVIII was restored to a fairly prosperous country, for although the wars of Napoleon had cut deeply into national resources material and human, the resilience of the French people and particularly the beneficial land distribution introduced by the Revolution brought about rapid economic recovery. The Charter of 1814 provided a constitutional monarchy somewhat similar to the system in Great Britain, although with greater powers in the hands of the king. But the bitterness of factional spirit prevented this constitutional system from functioning smoothly. On the one hand were the Ultra-Royalists, former émigrés and their children, greedy for revenge and the reëstablishment of their privileges, and contemptuous of the mild liberalism of the Charter; on the other hand were the Republicans and Bonapartists, bitter at the restoration of the king and the defeat of the Revolution. These irreconcilable groups kept politics in an uproar, although it is probable that the majority of the nation was willing to accept any compromise that would preserve quiet.

In the first year of the restoration (1815-1816) the Ultra-Royalists dominated the Chamber of Deputies and instituted a fierce reaction marked by rioting and proscriptions (the White Terror). From 1816 to 1820 a more moderate government, led by the King and Elie Decazes, maintained order and governed in the spirit of the Charter. But in 1820, following the assassination of the King's nephew, the Duke of Berry, a new Ultra-Royalist reaction undid the conciliating work of the preceding four years. The press was muzzled, the civil rights guaranteed by the Charter were suspended, a police espionage was established, and the property qualification for voters was raised. In 1823 a French army, led by the Duke of Angoulême, intervened in Spain to crush the liberal movement in that country. Upon the death of Louis XVIII (1824) his brother, Count of Artois, became king as Charles X. A stanch reactionary, Charles X, with the aid of the Ultra-Royalist Chamber, granted an indemnity ($200,-000,000) to the émigrés for the land they had lost. He also allowed the return of the Jesuits and continued the policy of entrusting public education entirely to the clergy. But his policies gradually alienated large groups, and in 1827 the Ultra-Royalists lost their majority in the Chamber of Deputies. Particularly irritating to the bourgeoisie was Charles' device for raising the immense indemnification for the émigrés. He reduced interest payments on the public debt and applied the savings thus made to annuities to the émigrés. This meant that payment was to be made directly from the pockets of government bond-holders, i.e., the bourgeoisie. By 1830 liberal dissatisfaction with the rule of Charles X had reached a boiling point.

Spain and Liberalism. In Spain the liberal Constitution of 1812 was revoked by Ferdinand VII upon his restoration. A thoroughly reactionary policy was substituted. This served to bring about a revolt in 1820 and a short-lived triumph for liberalism (1820-1822). Metternich assembled the Powers of the Quadruple Alliance at Verona (1822) to discuss the Spanish revolt and arrange for its suppression. At this conference, which was attended by France as well as the Powers of the Quadruple Alliance, it was decided that France would intervene in Spain under a general mandate of the Powers. Great Britain refused to support this scheme but did not attempt forcibly to resist it. A French army invaded Spain in 1823 and after much fighting, forced the Liberals out of Madrid into Cadiz, where they fortified themselves with Ferdinand, a prisoner. Ferdinand was released upon promising to establish a moderate government. Once safe, however, Ferdinand repudiated his promises and once more set the wheels in motion to crush liberalism. The reaction of 1824 was much more intense than that of 1814. Even the Duke of Angoulême, the leader of the French invading army, protested against Ferdinand's excesses. Reaction and absolutism, with every refinement of stupid and treacherous cruelty, remained supreme in Spain until Ferdinand's death in 1833, after which a bloody and destructive civil war kept Spain in an uproar for many years.

During the long period of war and disorder (beginning in 1808 with Napoleon's interference in Spanish affairs) the Spanish colonies in South America had been in revolt. By 1823 most of them had succeeded in establishing independent governments. It would have been thoroughly in accord with the policies of Metternich and the Quadruple Alliance for the European Powers to have suppressed the South American revolt, but this could not be done without the active assistance of British sea-power. The leading British statesmen, Castlereagh and (after 1822) Canning, while unsympathetic with revolution, considered that British economic interests would be best served by an independent South America, and accordingly Great Britain refused to coöperate with the Metternich policies. In 1823 James Monroe, President of the United States, having reached an understanding with Canning, proclaimed the famous Monroe Doctrine, which asserted that the United States would consider it an act of aggression for any country to colonize further in, or otherwise to interfere with, the new republics of South America. The Monroe Doctrine, supported by both Britain and the United States, made the extension of Metternichism to the New World quite hopeless.

Portugal and Liberalism. While the Portuguese royal family found refuge from Napoleon in Brazil (1807-1820), Great Britain was virtually in control of the country. The British occupation was resented both by patriotic reactionaries and by Liberals. In 1820, during a temporary absence of the British governor, the Portuguese army, largely inspired by the contemporaneous revolt in Spain, got control of the government and with the help of the Liberals formulated a constitution similar to Spain's. King John VI returned from Brazil in 1822 and accepted the constitution. In that year Brazil broke away from Portugal and made John VI's son, Pedro I, Emperor. Don Miguel, another son, led the reactionaries against the constitutional government. When the French invaded Spain in 1823, John VI revoked the constitution but succeeded only in incensing the Liberals without satisfying the reactionaries. Don Miguel continued his agitation. In 1826 John VI died, and Pedro I of Brazil became Pedro IV of Portugal. Pedro, a man of liberal sympathies, granted a charter providing for parliamentary government. He then abdicated his Portuguese crown in favor of his seven year old daughter Maria, with the understanding that she should marry Don Miguel. Miguel, who had been banished by his father in 1824, now returned as regent (1828). Disregarding his solemn promises to support the constitution of Pedro, Miguel introduced a savage despotism. His excesses continued until his deposition in 1834.

Great Britain and Liberalism. Great Britain's desire to curb the commercial expansion of Spain and Portugal and to cut in on the South American trade had led her to support the Monroe Doctrine and to refuse to coöperate with Metternich's program of foreign interference to crush liberalism. But in her domestic policies during the period 1815-1822, Great Britain was quite as reactionary as Metternich himself. Throughout the French Revolutionary epoch (1789-1815), the fear of the spread of radical French ideas was a bugbear of the British governing classes. Although England had established a parliamentary monarchy in the seventeenth century and was thus regarded as "liberal" by the philosophers of the eighteenth century, she had actually made hardly more progress toward democracy by 1789 than had the absolute monarchies of the continent. A tight little oligarchy of landed aristocrats entirely controlled the government, and although there was a long tradition of civil rights under the law and of freedom of the press, the British aristocrats were quite as capable as those of any other country of enacting repressive measures as soon as their privileges seemed threatened by popular agitation. In 1815 the Tory cabinet, fresh from its triumph over Napoleon and the French Revolution, was less inclined than ever to offer any measures of reform in a liberal direction. The period 1815-1822 was marked by an extreme conservatism. King George IV, Castlereagh, and Wellington championed reaction. The Tory House of Commons passed legislation favorable to their class interests (increased duties on the importation of grain; continuing Enclosure Acts; abolition of the Income Tax), while acute economic distress among the lower classes went unrelieved.

In 1816 the discontent of the unemployed workingmen found expression in a formidable series of riots culminating in the Spafields Riot in London. In 1817, frightened by continuing disturbances, the government suspended the Habeas Corpus Act, the principal bulwark of English civil liberty. In 1819 there was renewed agitation, and a great mass-meeting at Manchester was broken up by the soldiers of the government with some bloodshed. This "Manchester Massacre" resulted in the passage of a group of severely repressive measures known as the "Six Acts." In spite of its outward appearance of success, however, the British reaction was being rapidly undermined by a strong liberal movement. The liberal opposition came from (1) intellectual radicals—William Godwin, Thomas Paine, William Cobbett, Jeremy Bentham, Percy Bysshe Shelley, and Lord Byron, (2) Roman Catholics, particularly in Ireland, who were clamoring for the repeal of the laws denying political office to members of their faith, (3) Protestant dissenters, who objected to the preferential treatment accorded to Anglicans in politics, taxation, and higher education, and (4) the rising industrial capitalists, or bourgeoisie. Because the Industrial Revolution was well advanced in England by 1815, these last formed a powerful body whom in the long run it would be impossible to oppose. During the decade 1822-1832 this liberal movement gained considerable strength in spite of the stubborn stand-pattism of the conservatives. The liberal foreign policy of Canning was the first indication of the changing order. In 1825, through the instigation of Francis Place and William Huskisson, the act prohibiting combinations of workingmen (trade unions) was repealed. In 1828, by the repeal of the Corporation and Test Acts, Protestant dissenters were admitted to political office. In the following year, the Catholic Relief Act removed the civil disabilities of Catholics. A strong movement, now supported by important men in the cabinet, had developed favoring Parliamentary Reform—extension of the franchise to the middle class and redistribution of seats in Parliament to give representation proportioned to population.

Russia under Alexander I. Alexander I of Russia came to the Congress of Vienna with many liberal ideas. He had granted constitutional charters to Finland and to Poland, and he had taken a considerable share in drawing up the Charter of 1814 that Louis XVIII had granted to France. Under the influence of Metternich, however, Alexander gradually became converted to reaction. Of all the great European countries, Russia was the most backward educationally and industrially and thus the least fitted for democratic reform. These considerations, the discovery of an assassination conspiracy among the officers of his guard, the uprising of 1820 in Spain and Italy, all contributed to Alexander's change of heart. In 1820 Alexander admitted to Metternich that liberalism was both a failure and a source of danger, and from that time on he coöperated vigorously with the Austrian Chancellor's anti-liberal war.

Central Europe Controlled by Metternich. In central Europe, Metternichism was supreme. All the engines of suppression that his ingenuity could devise were set in motion by Metternich against everything that savored of innovation or freedom. Rigid control of the press and of education, and omnipresent police surveillance were the orders of the day. Not only in Austria, but also in the Germanies and in Italy, Metternich watched for any flare-up and then rushed to smother it. Some promises of liberal reform made by the princes in the Germanies were not carried out. Manifestations of the liberal undercurrent broke out in secret societies, the Burschenschaft and the Wartburg Festival (1817). The Carlsbad Decrees (1819) were the government's answer to these subversive movements. In Italy, Metternich's power was felt from Lombardy and Venetia to the Kingdom of the Two Sicilies. On the surface reaction was firmly entrenched, but liberalism, though driven to cover, still lived. Secret societies (the most important known as the *Carbonari*) were supported by many. As they had done in Portugal and Spain, the Liberals rose up in 1820 and were successful in forcing the promise of a constitution from the king. But as a result of Metternich's conferences at Troppau and Laibach, Austrian intervention was sanctioned, the revolution was stamped out by force, and the constitution was abolished.

DECLINE OF METTERNICHISM (1822-1830)

Non-coöperation of Great Britain. One of the major reasons for the decline of Metternichism and its eventual failure was the foreign policy of non-intervention adopted by Great Britain after 1822. Canning and other British leaders were chiefly influenced in withdrawing from the Metternich system by the desire of promoting British commercial interests rather than by philosophical adherence to liberal principles.

The Greek Revolution. A second cause that worked powerfully to undermine Metternichism was the Greek War of Independence against the Turks, which started in 1821 with an uprising in Moldavia. Though personally sympathetic toward the Greek cause and anxious to see a diminution of the dangerous Turkish power, Tsar Alexander was persuaded by Metternich not to intervene. It was supposed that without foreign help the Greeks would be quickly crushed. The Greeks, however, displayed a heroic national spirit, while the barbarous methods employed by the Turks to put down the rebellion created a revulsion of feeling throughout Europe. Intellectuals and romantics (Lord Byron, Victor Hugo, Wilhelm Müller, and others) took up the Greek cause. After the death of Tsar Alexander (1825), Metternich was no longer able to exercise a decisive influence in Russian affairs, while sympathy for the Greeks and hatred of the Turks were growing throughout Russia. In 1827 the new Tsar, Nicholas I, joined with Great Britain and France, and signed the Treaty of London by which it was agreed that these Powers would intervene to force an armistice in Greece to be followed, presumably, by some sort of compromise on the question of independence. The Turks refused to accept an armistice, and the new allies destroyed the Turkish-Egyptian fleet in the Bay of Navarino (1827). The following year Russia declared war on Turkey. For France and Russia to aid a country in throwing off its "legitimate" rulers was a bitter pill for Metternich. In 1829 the Turks were defeated and forced to accept the Treaty of Adrianople, which acknowledged Greek independence.

Revolutions of 1830. By 1830 discontent with reaction and suppression of nationalistic aspirations had reached explosive proportions in many parts of Europe. In France, Charles X published his July Ordinances (1) restricting further the freedom of the press, (2) dissolving the new Chamber to which a liberal majority had been elected, (3) promulgating a new electoral law narrowing the suffrage, and (4) calling for new elections, which would presumably result in the return of a reactionary majority. Secretly financed and directed by the leaders of the bourgeoisie (bankers, factory-owners, and merchants), a revolt broke out in Paris; armed bands of workingmen barricaded the streets and easily defeated the king's soldiers, who were themselves largely in sympathy with the rioters. Charles X abdicated and fled to England. Louis Philippe, Duke of Orleans, was made king under a constitutional system that placed effective control in the hands of the bourgeoisie. The success of this "July Revolution" in France brought immediate repercussions in other parts of Europe. The Belgians revolted from the Dutch and declared their independence in October 1831, an independence recognized by France and Great Britain the following year. In Italy, the Papal states rose against the Pope, and Parma and Modena forced their Hapsburg rulers to flee to Vienna. But Metternich soon crushed these uprisings and restored the old system. Liberalism was not yet strong enough in central Europe to overthrow Metternichism. The Polish revolt in 1831 was severely put down by Nicholas I. The Revolutions of 1830 marked the end of the first phase of the struggle between liberalism and reaction that formed the leading political issue of the nineteenth century. Metternich had retarded liberalism but had failed to eradicate the influence of the French Revolution.

CHAPTER XVIII.

THE GROWTH OF LIBERALISM

In England and France the period 1830-1848 was preëminently the Era of the Bourgeoisie. Commerce and Industry were in the saddle. In central and eastern Europe, where the Industrial Revolution had not yet penetrated deeply, the period was still the Era of Metternichism with its feudal survivals and political absolutism. During the whole period international diplomacy was in the background and internal social problems were of paramount importance. Outstanding features were the sharpening of the division lines between rich and poor, partly as a result of the rise of industrial capitalism and partly as a result of the decreasing docility and ignorance of the working class. What Edwin Markham has called "the long, long patience of the plundered poor" was beginning to wear out. Increasing numbers of men became converted to the ideas of democracy, which had been opposed even by advanced liberals in the period 1815-1830. Yet in most countries, government remained unresponsive, in general, to public opinion, and thus a dangerous dissatisfaction, unable to find vent in peaceful political activity, was gradually building up to the *ultima ratio* of revolution. Three distinct movements contributed to this dissatisfaction: (1) the movement for national self-determination (Italian states, Hungary, Poland, Ireland); (2) the movement for social and economic betterment among the submerged masses (France, England); and (3) the movement toward democracy (France, England) and toward constitutionalism (Austria, German states). In 1848, touched off by the February Revolution at Paris, all Europe exploded like a firecracker. Although the revolutions of 1848 failed to realize a fraction of the hopes of their supporters, they marked the end almost everywhere of the era of stand-pattism and ushered in an era of change.

REFORMS IN GREAT BRITAIN

Growth of Religious Tolerance. Until 1689 England, like most other European countries, attempted to enforce religious uniformity by law. The Corporation Act (1661) and the Test Act (1673) denied public office to all who refused to disavow transubstantiation and to receive the sacrament according to the rites of the Church of England. Other laws of the sixteenth and seventeenth centuries imposed heavy penalties on public worship of Roman Catholics and Protestant dissenters. The Toleration Act (1689) permitted dissenters to worship publicly but continued to exclude them from public office and the universities. In the eighteenth century there was a great growth of the spirit of toleration and even a considerable flourishing of deistic and atheistic opinion, and at the beginning of the nineteenth century the Test and Corporation Acts had become essentially political rather than religious measures. In 1828, yielding to the general agitation for liberalizing reforms, Parliament repealed the disabling acts as far as they related to dissenters. Roman Catholics continued under the ban. In 1829, influenced chiefly by the threatening state of affairs in Ireland, where Daniel O'Connell had become a powerful Catholic leader, the Tory government, led by the Duke of Wellington and Robert Peel, sponsored the Catholic Relief Bill which abolished the ancient Oath of Supremacy and the declaration against transubstantiation and thus allowed Catholics to occupy seats in Parliament and hold most positions in the government. Finally, in 1858, a further reform threw open public office to Jews.

Parliamentary Reform (1832). The demand for the extension of suffrage and for the redistribution of seats in Parliament to conform with the distribution of population (referred to by the specific term, Parliamentary Reform) was a result of the Industrial Revolution and the rise of the industrial middle class. The Whig party championed reform in order to win the support of the middle classes. After much opposition from the House of Lords, which was overborne only by the threat of creating new peers, the Reform Bill was finally passed in 1832. It provided for the disfranchisement of forty-one boroughs of negligible population ("rotten boroughs"), for the partial disfranchisement of thirty more boroughs, and for the allocation of the seats thus released to the large new industrial cities. The property qualification for voting was broadened rather than reduced, i.e., other kinds of property than freeheld land were taken into account as qualification. This extension increased the number of voters from about 3 per cent to about 5 per cent of the whole population. Practically no concession, therefore, was made to democracy. The Reform Bill further stipulated that all voting must be done in two days instead of fifteen. A serious weakness of the Reform Bill was its failure to provide for vote by ballot, so that it remained possible for powerful men to control many votes. The Reform Bill brought about a re-alignment of the old political parties; the Whigs and many of the new capitalists began to call themselves Liberals; and the Tories, giving up many of their old traditions under the leadership of Robert Peel and accepting into their ranks such of the new business men as wished to proceed with change slowly, began to call themselves Conservatives.

Chartism. The reform of 1832 had been vigorously supported by the working class, but they soon discovered that no benefits whatever accrued to them from its passage. Indeed, the new group of bourgeoisie who had secured political power by the Reform Bill were less sensitive to the needs of the lower classes than the land-owning aristocracy that they replaced. They were wedded to the ideas of laissez faire and free competition, and they were quite free from any sentimental nonsense about political and social privileges carrying with them any responsibility except that of growing rich. Disappointed at receiving a stone for bread, the lower classes began to agitate for something more substantial than the right to make contracts freely at starvation wages in unsanitary factories. This lower-class agitation crystallized around a program for political reform known as the "People's Charter." The program demanded (1) universal manhood suffrage, (2) vote by secret ballot, (3) annual Parliaments, (4) equal electoral districts, (5) removal of property qualification for members of Parliament, and (6) salary payment of members of Parliament. All the objectives of the Chartists except the unimportant point (3) have since been attained in Great Britain. They may seem to modern eyes a temperate expression of the minimum requirements for a democratic government, but in 1838, when first proposed, they were regarded as violently revolutionary, and they found very few defenders among educated and "respectable" men. From 1838 to 1848 Chartism was vigorously agitated in England, but no concessions to it were made by the government. It was regarded throughout as a subversive and incendiary movement to be put down by force. The movement finally collapsed in 1848 when a much advertised gigantic mass-meeting on Kennington Common in London was attended by a comparative handful who were easily dispersed by the police. Although it failed to accomplish any immediate results, the Chartist agitation served to focus the attention of many of England's ablest minds on what Thomas Carlyle called "the condition-of-England-question" and so paved the way for far-reaching political reforms in the last half of the century.

Social Legislation (1832-1848). The period 1832-1848 saw the beginning of much social reform legislation in England. Most of it was pushed through an apathetic or hostile Parliament by the ceaseless effort of a small group of humanitarians. From the modern point of view the total accomplishment seems small, but the foundations were laid for more effective reform in the future. In 1833, through the efforts of Michael Sadler and Lord Ashley, the first important Factory Act was passed. The law limited child labor in specified industries. Although no adequate provision was made for its enforcement, the law was a great break with the naked doctrine of laissez faire. It was bitterly opposed by the capitalists, who gloomily predicted the ruin of British industry as a consequence of government interference. More advanced Factory Acts were passed in 1842, 1844, and 1847. A beginning was also made in 1833 of government support of elementary education. Negro slavery was abolished in the colonies by an act providing gradual emancipation with financial compensation to slaveholders. Less humanitarian and more hard-headed was the New Poor Law (1834) abolishing "outdoor relief" of the poor and establishing a system of workhouses where conditions were deliberately made as harsh as possible to discourage malingering.

Foreign Affairs (1830-1848). During most of this period British foreign policy was directed by the energetic and aggressive Lord Palmerston. In 1831 Palmerston supported the independence of Belgium, which had just revolted from the Dutch, and thus prevented that country from being annexed by France. In 1839 the permanent independence and neutrality of Belgium was guaranteed by all the important powers. In Spain from 1833 to 1838 a political struggle, frequently flaring out in civil war, was carried on between the partisans of Isabella, daughter of Ferdinand VII, and those of Don Carlos, Ferdinand's younger brother. Palmerston and Louis Philippe of France attempted to settle this Spanish broil to the advantage of their respective countries, but they frequently worked at cross purposes, and the net result of their schemes and counter-schemes was an estrangement between England and France. More important than Palmerston's Spanish interference was his policy toward affairs in the Near East. In 1832 a war broke out between Mehemet Ali, the Pasha of Egypt, and the Turks. The Turks called upon Russia for help, in return for which they promised to close the strategic Dardanelles to foreign warships whenever the Tsar was at war. Palmerston was ultimately successful in preventing this agreement from becoming effective, and he thus made the maintenance of the integrity of the Ottoman Empire and the neutralization of the Black Sea straits a cardinal aim of British policy.

FRANCE UNDER LOUIS PHILIPPE

Bourgeois Character of the July Monarchy. The Revolution of 1830 that established the "July Monarchy" of Louis Philippe was not a widespread popular uprising. It was rather a *coup d'état* engineered by a small group of moneyed bourgeoisie who took advantage of the discontent of the Paris workingmen to effect a political, not a social, revolution. The government they established was less democratic than that established in Great Britain by the Reform of 1832 and was to an even greater extent a class interest government by and for business and industry. High property qualifications kept the total number of electors to less than 250,000 in a population of 30,000,000. The government was "parliamentary" and "responsible" as in England, and the original intention was that the king should reign but should not govern. For various reasons, however, chief among which was the absence in France of a long parliamentary tradition, Louis Philippe was able to assume a much more dominating position than that occupied by William IV or Victoria. In practice the constitutional monarchy gradually developed into an absolutism controlled by the King and his able minister Guizot. Setting their faces against all reform or change, Louis Philippe and Guizot were forced to adopt more and more reactionary policies to suppress growing dissatisfaction.

Opposition to Louis Philippe. Numerous groups in France had grievances against the "July Monarchy." The Legitimists still insisted that Charles X, and later the Count of Chambord, was the rightful king. The Republicans, although they had aided Louis Philippe in securing the crown, were angered by his failure to introduce democratic reforms. Social reformers of various creeds denounced the government for failing to ameliorate the condition of the working classes. Patriots were humiliated by Louis Philippe's unaggressive foreign policy, his willingness to truckle to England, and his dismissal of his Foreign Minister, Adolphe Thiers, when that statesman attempted to assert France's interests at the risk of war. The prevalence of graft in the conduct of the government of Guizot furnished opportunities for disaffected journalists to attack the régime and led to reprisals in the form of press censorship, which served only to drive the opposition underground without appeasing it. Alexis de Tocqueville summed up the various elements of discontent in a speech in the Chamber of Deputies, January 29, 1848: "See what is passing in the breasts of the working classes,—who, I grant, are at present quiet. No doubt they are not disturbed by political passion, properly so called, to the same extent that they have been; but can you not see that their passions, instead of political, have become social? Do you not see that there are gradually forming in their breasts opinions and ideas that are destined to upset not only this or that ministry, law or form of government, but society itself, until it totters upon the foundations on which it rests today? Do you not listen to what they say to themselves each day? Do you not hear them repeating unceasingly that all that is above them is unworthy and incapable; that the present distribution of goods throughout the world is unjust; that property rests on a foundation that is not equitable? And do you not realize that when such opinions take root, when they spread in an almost universal manner, when they sink deeply into the masses, they are bound to bring with them sooner or later, I know not when or how, a most formidable revolution?"

The February Revolution (1848). Louis Philippe, Guizot, and the bourgeois Chamber of Deputies could not see, as de Tocqueville saw, the real drift of affairs. They persisted in their policy of suppression and no reform. Because censorship of the press made dissemination of political opinions through ordinary channels impossible, the opponents of the government had developed a practice of attending "banquets" where radical views were expressed and plans for coercing the government were discussed. The chief reform contemplated by these intellectual radicals was democratic extension of the suffrage. In February 1848 the government attempted to prevent one of these banquets. This proved a signal for the outbreak of rioting in different parts of Paris, and when Guizot attempted to restore order by the use of the National Guard, many of the soldiers refused to obey their officers. In a riot in front of Guizot's home, fifty demonstrators were killed or wounded, and this bloodshed further infuriated the revolutionaries. After a futile attempt to make terms with the rioters, Louis Philippe abdicated and made his escape to England. Amid great disorder a provisional government, headed by the Catholic liberal and poet, Lamartine, but including almost every shade of political and social opinion, was selected. The provisional government decreed a general election under universal manhood suffrage for members of a National Assembly to draw up a constitution.

The Second Republic and the Socialists. The provisional government remained in control for four months pending the election of the new Assembly. Pressed by the desperate economic necessities of the unemployed proletariat in Paris and led by the socialist theorist Louis Blanc, the government undertook to guarantee the "right to work" and agreed to employ on public works ("national workshops"), at a wage of two francs a day, all who were unemployed. As the government could not immediately organize productive work for the large numbers who applied, the national workshop idea of Louis Blanc actually developed into a simple dole from the public funds. The number of those who drew this dole rose alarmingly, and conservatives all over the country became terrified. In the elections to the National Assembly, the socialists were snowed under, and one of the first acts of the National Assembly (June 1848) was the abolition of the "abominable" national workshop system. The unemployed workingmen, thus suddenly cut off from the government subsidy they had been enjoying, rose in revolt but were mercilessly crushed by the soldiers of the National Assembly under General Cavaignac in the terribly bloody "June Days" (June 24-26, 1848).

The Second Republic and the Bourgeoisie. Having violently suppressed the social revolt of the working class, the new Assembly, controlled by bourgeois Republicans and conservatives from the agricultural districts, adopted a constitution providing for a single chamber legislature and a president to be elected for four years by universal suffrage. Moderate political reforms were adopted. Capital punishment for purely political offenses was abolished. The right of association and public meeting was guaranteed. While the obligation of the government to furnish work for the unemployed was specifically repudiated, a statement was included in the constitution that the government would assist the unemployed "as far as its resources permitted."

ITALY AND THE REVOLUTION OF 1848

Opposition to Austrian Dominion. Throughout the period 1830-1848 a strong undercurrent of opposition was developing in Italy toward the despotism of Austria and the independent Hapsburg rulers. Mazzini's secret society favored a republic; the Clericals agitated for a federation under the Pope; a third group looked to the liberal Charles Albert, King of Sardinia, as the rallying point for an Italian *risorgimento*. In many centers outside Italy, notably Marseilles, groups of political exiles banded together in a formidable society, "Young Italy." Characteristic of the Italian liberal movement were its intense nationalism and its comparative indifference to the social and economic issues that the Industrial Revolution had infused into the liberalism of England and France.

National Uprising (1848).   In March 1848 rebellion against the Austrians broke out in Milan. After several days of desperate fighting the Austrian army, under Field-marshal Radetzky, was driven out of the city. The rest of Lombardy and Venetia immediately joined the revolt. Charles Albert, King of Sardinia and Piedmont, now declared war against Austria and came to the aid of the revolutionists with a disciplined army. In the Kingdom of the Two Sicilies (Southern Italy) a constitutional government had been set up, while in the Papal States the liberal Pius IX was definitely sympathetic to the Italian national aspirations. For a short time (May and June 1848) it appeared that the uprising, headed by the Piedmontese army of Charles Albert, would be successful in throwing the Austrians permanently out of the whole peninsula. But on July 25, Radetzky defeated Charles Albert at the decisive battle of Custozza and reoccupied Milan.

Restoration of Austrian Control.   The following year (1849) Charles Albert made a further effort, but was defeated by Radetzky at Novara. Charles Albert then abdicated the throne of Sardinia in favor of his son Victor Emmanuel. The Austrians recaptured all the revolted territory, but sowed the seeds of intense hatred by the cruelty with which General Haynau punished the city of Brescia. Although the attempts of the Italian patriots were thus unsuccessful in 1848-1849, an inspiring example had been set, and there remained, as a powerful gathering ground for a future effort, the constitutional monarchy of Sardinia and Piedmont under the able, liberal, and intensely Italian-minded Victor Emmanuel II.

GERMANY AND THE REVOLUTION OF 1848

Underground Liberal Movements (1830-1848).   In Germany, as throughout central Europe, Metternichism continued to rule throughout the period 1830-1848. The Industrial Revolution was just beginning its corrosive influence on the social order represented by the old régime. Bourgeoisie and urban workingmen were still not numerous enough to challenge effectively the power of the landed aristocracy. Economic liberalism, therefore, that had been the real motive power behind the Paris revolution of 1830 and the British Reform of 1832, was largely lacking in Germany. But intellectual and political liberalism, the inheritance of the French rather than the Industrial Revolution, gained headway in spite of Metternich and his secret police, in spite of censorship of the press and of education, and in spite of the strict system of passports designed to prevent the infiltration of radical persons and ideas from abroad. The universities, in particular, became dangerous centers of liberal agitation.

The Frankfurt Assembly (1848). When news of the February revolution at Paris reached Germany, there were simultaneous uprisings in many German cities. Most of the German states demanded a constitutional monarchy, a free press, and a strong Germanic federation. In Baden, Bavaria, Saxony, and Hanover, and in the independent Hanse towns the frightened German princes installed liberal ministries and promised to grant constitutions. Serious rioting broke out in Berlin, and Frederick William IV of Prussia was forced to appoint a liberal ministry and convoke a constituent assembly. In May 1848 an assembly representing all the German states convened at Frankfurt with the intention of drawing up a constitution for the entire German confederation. For nearly a year this assembly deliberated and wrangled; finally, in 1849 it completed the drawing up of a constitution providing a limited monarchy and a union of all the German states. The crown of this proposed united German Empire was offered to Frederick William IV of Prussia. But a reaction against liberalism had set in, and although Frederick William was tempted by the dream of a united Germany under Prussian leadership, his hatred of constitutionalism led him to decline the offer. The Frankfurt Assembly then broke up; its more radical leaders fled the country.

Reaction in Prussia. In the fall of 1848 the tide of liberalism was fast ebbing in Prussia and throughout the Germanies. The failure of the liberals to hold their gains arose from the fact that their movement was the work of a minority of enthusiasts; the bulk of the nation remained apathetic if not strongly conservative. Frederick William IV soon felt himself strong enough to dismiss the liberal ministry he had appointed during the March crisis, and he appointed Count Brandenburg, a stanch reactionary, to administer the government. The Berlin populace was easily cowed by a display of military force. A constitution, indeed, was granted as promised, but it was drawn up by Frederick William himself and his own advisers and contained nothing liberal save empty gestures. A similar reaction occurred in the other German states. Scattered efforts of the liberals continued after the dissolution of the Frankfurt Assembly (May 1849), but they were easily suppressed by Prussian troops. Many political refugees emigrated to the United States. Many more were caught and jailed.

REVOLUTION IN THE AUSTRIAN EMPIRE

Vienna. In Vienna, the capital of Metternichism, dissatisfaction had long been brewing. Revolutionary news from France and Italy precipitated violent rioting (March 13-15, 1848). Metternich resigned his ministry and fled for his life. The weak and helpless Ferdinand I immediately offered liberal concessions; the press censorship was revoked and a constitution was promised.

Bohemia and Hungary. The heterogeneous population in the Hapsburg empire greatly complicated the issues of the revolutionary movement of 1848. As soon as they saw that the Vienna government was shaking, nationalist patriots in Bohemia and Hungary began revolts the object of which, like that of the Italian revolt, was national autonomy rather than any liberalization of the Austrian imperial government. Because of this diversification of aims, there was no coöperation among the liberals in Bohemia, Hungary, and Italy. This disunity in the revolting forces enabled the imperial government to deal with them separately. In June 1848 a Pan-Slavic Congress convened at Prague with the intention of drawing up an independent government for the Czechs, Slovaks, and other Slavic peoples within the Austrian Empire. This movement was quickly crushed by the soldiers of Prince Windischgrätz. More serious was the revolt of the Hungarians. Led by the able and patriotic Louis Kossuth, the Hungarians set up an autonomous state with freedom of the press, abolition of privilege, and annual Diets, and extended the franchise to the middle class (owners of property worth about $1000).

Reaction under Francis Joseph. Having successfully put down the revolt at Prague, the army under Prince Windischgrätz marched on Vienna (October 1848), and after several days of fighting succeeded in capturing the city and restoring the authority of the Emperor. An attempt was made by the Hungarians to save the Vienna revolutionaries, but the relieving army was beaten back, and the only result of the effort was that a more severe punishment was meted out by the victorious Windischgrätz. Immediately after the capture of Vienna, the Emperor Ferdinand abdicated in favor of his nephew Francis Joseph. The real power of the re-established imperial government, however, was Prince Felix Schwartzenberg, a man whose methods and ideas, if not his abilities, were nearly indistinguishable from those of Prince Metternich. As the year 1848 came to a close, it was evident that the revolution, so far as it regarded the internal government of Austria, had failed; reaction was again firmly entrenched. It remained to be seen whether the revolting Italians and Hungarians would be able to make good their efforts at independence. In 1849 this question was answered adversely for both revolting nationalities. The Italians were first defeated, and with the troops thus released the Austrians attacked the Hungarians in earnest. The Tsar came to the help of his brother emperor with an army of 80,000 Russians. Against the overwhelming force of their enemies the Hungarians had no chance; after three months of desperate but hopeless resistance they were compelled to surrender. The notorious General Haynau inflicted a savage punishment on the captured leaders. Louis Kossuth and a few others escaped to Turkey. With the collapse of the Hungarian Republic the Austrian revolution of 1848-1849 came to an end; the dominions of the Hapsburgs remained intact; Metternich was gone, but in his place was his replica, Schwartzenberg; practically all the reforms and concessions except the abolition of serfdom were repudiated. Nevertheless, the revolution had shaken the monarchy to its foundation, and even its apparently complete suppression could never reconstruct the reactionary psychology of the heyday of Metternichism.

Chronology of
Significant Dates (1450-1963)*

1450-1559

1450-1455	First printing with movable type (Gutenberg at Mainz).
1453	Capture of Constantinople by Ottoman Turks.
1455-1485	Wars of the Roses (England).
1492	Conquest of Moors completed (Granada, Spain).
1492	Discovery of New World (Christopher Columbus).
1497-1498	Discovery of all-water route to India (Vasco da Gama).
1504	Spanish conquest of Naples.
1508	League of Cambrai (coalition against Venice).
1513	Discovery of Pacific Ocean (Nuñez de Balboa).
1517	Martin Luther denounces abuse of indulgences (95 Theses).
1518-1531	Huldreich Zwingli preaches reform doctrines at Geneva.
1519	Disputation at Leipzig (Luther vs. Johann von Eck).
1519-1522	Circumnavigation of globe (Ferdinand Magellan).
1521	Luther excommunicated. Diet of Worms.
1524-1525	Peasants' Revolt crushed in Germany.
1526	Hungarians crushed at Mohacs by Turks.
1527	Sack of Rome by Imperial troops.
1529	Term "Protestants" first used (Diet of Speier).
1529	Peace of Cambrai (Charles V and Francis I).
1530	Definitive Lutheran doctrine set forth (Confession of Augsburg).
1533-1556	Thomas Cranmer Archbishop of Canterbury.
1534	Act of Supremacy makes Henry VIII head of English Church.
1534	Order of Jesuits founded (Ignatius Loyola).
1535	*Institutes of the Christian Religion* (John Calvin)
1536-1564	Calvin at Geneva.
1543	*Revolutions of the Celestial Bodies* (Nicolaus Copernicus).
1545-1563	Council of Trent (Catholic Reformation).
1553-1558	Catholic reaction in England under Mary I.
1555	Religious peace of Augsburg. *"Cuius regio, eius religio."*
1555	Abdication of Charles V.
1559	Peace of Cateau-Cambrésis ending half a century of intermittent warfare between France and the Empire.

1559-1598

1559-1572	John Knox preaches Calvinism in Scotland.
1566	"League of Beggars" in Netherlands.
1571	Turks defeated at Lepanto (Don John of Austria).
1572	Massacre of St. Bartholomew's Day (Catherine de' Medici; Admiral de Coligny; Huguenots).
1576	Pacification of Ghent.
1579	Union of Utrecht.
1582	Gregorian Calendar.

* Refer to page 166 for dates for Chief European Rulers.

1587	Execution of Mary, Queen of Scots, in England.
1588	Defeat of Spanish Armada by English.
1589	Henry of Navarre (Bourbon) becomes Henry IV of France.
1598	Edict of Nantes. End of French religious wars.

1598-1648

1600-1610	Financial reforms of Sully.
1600	English East India Company chartered.
1614	Last meeting of Estates General in France previous to Revolution (Marie de' Medici).
1618-1648	Thirty Years' War.
1620	Sailing of *Mayflower*.
1624-1642	Ascendancy of Cardinal Richelieu in France.
1625	Huguenot insurrection in France.
1628	Petition of Right accepted by Charles I of England.
1629	Peace of Lübeck. Edict of Restitution (return of confiscated lands to Catholic Church).
1632	Battle of Lützen. Victory and death of Gustavus Adolphus.
1636	John Hampden refuses payment of ship-money in England.
1640-1660	Long Parliament in England.
1642-1646	Civil war in England. "Great Rebellion."
1643-1661	Cardinal Mazarin in power in France.
1648	Peace of Westphalia. General settlement of European affairs after Thirty Years' War.

1648-1715

1648-1653	Disturbances of Fronde in France.
1649	Trial and Execution of Charles I of England.
1653-1658	Unopposed rule of Oliver Cromwell.
1659	Peace of the Pyrenees (France, Spain). Marriage of Louis XIV with Spanish Infanta. Renunciation of French claims on Spanish crown.
1660	Restoration of monarchy in England (Charles II).
1667-1668	War of Devolution (Louis XIV).
1672-1678	Dutch War (Louis XIV).
1679	Habeas Corpus Act (England).
1685	Revocation of Edict of Nantes. Persecution and emigration of Huguenots.
1686	League of Augsburg formed against Louis XIV.
1687	*Principia* (Isaac Newton).
1688	"Glorious Revolution" in England.
1689	Declaration of Right (Bill of Rights) in England.
1689-1697	War of the League of Augsburg (or Palatinate) (Louis XIV).
1697	Peace of Ryswick.
1700	Death of Charles II of Spain precipitates struggle over partition of Spanish dominions.
1700-1721	Great Northern War (Charles XII, Peter I and allies).
1701	Frederick of Brandenburg takes title of King of Prussia.
1702-1713	War of Spanish Succession (Grand Alliance, Louis XIV).
1704	Battle of Blenheim (Marlborough and Prince Eugene defeat French).
1707	Act of Union (England, Scotland).
1709	Battle of Poltava (Peter I defeats Charles XII).
1713	Peace of Utrecht-Rastadt. General settlement of War of Spanish Succession.
1715	Death of Louis XIV.

1715-1789

1720	Speculative fever. Mississippi scheme of John Law in France, South Sea Bubble in England.
1748	*Spirit of the Laws* (Montesquieu).
1752	Publication of *Encyclopedia* begun (Diderot).
1756	"Black Hole of Calcutta."
1756-1763	Seven Years' War (England against France, Prussia against Austria, France, and Russia).
1757	Battle of Plassey. Robert Clive master of Bengal.
1757-1761	Ascendancy of William Pitt in England.
1759	Capture of Quebec (Wolfe defeats Montcalm).
1760	End of French power in India.
1761	*The Social Contract* (J. J. Rousseau).
1762	Death of Elizabeth of Russia turns scale of war on continent in favor of Frederick the Great.
1762-1796	Catherine II, the Great, of Russia.
1763	Peace of Paris. Settlement of Seven Years' War.
1765	Stamp Act arouses antagonism in British colonies.
1768	Annexation of Corsica to France.
1768-1774	Russo-Turkish War. Russia obtains footing on Black Sea.
1772	First partition of Poland.
1774-1776	Attempted reforms of Turgot.
1776	American Declaration of Independence.
1776	*Wealth of Nations* (Adam Smith).
1777	Defeat of Burgoyne by Americans at Saratoga.
1778	France joins American colonists against England.
1780	Russia, Denmark, Sweden in Armed Neutrality in English-French war.
1781	Capitulation of Yorktown.
1781	*Compte Rendu* (Jacques Necker).
1783	Peace of Paris. American independence recognized.
1783-1787	Calonne, Minister of Finance in France. Increasing financial difficulties.
1787	French Assembly of Notables refuses to accept taxation reform.
1788	Opposition of French parlements. Summoning of Estates General.
1789	Beginning of French Revolution.

1789-1815

1789	Estates General met at Versailles (May 5).
1789	Third Estate forms National Assembly (Mirabeau, Sieyes) (June 20-27).
1789	Revolt of Paris. Storming of Bastille (Camille Desmoulins) (July 12-14).
1789	Abolition of feudal privileges (July-August).
1791	Constitution of 1791. Limited monarchy.
1791	Declaration of Pillnitz (Frederick William II, Leopold III) (August).
1792	Invasion of France stopped at Valmy (Dumouriez, Kellerman), (September 20).
1792-1797	War between France and the First Coalition (April).
1792	National Convention meets, abolishes monarchy (September 21).
1792-1793	Trial and execution of Louis XVI.
1793	War declared against Great Britain, Holland, Spain.
1793-1794	Dictatorship of Committee of Public Safety (Danton, Robespierre, St. Just, Couthon).

1793	Second partition of Poland.
1793-1794	Reign of Terror.
1794	Polish revolt crushed (Kosciuszko).
1795	Constitution of the Year III (France).
1795	Beginning of government of Directory (1795-1799).
1795	Final partition of Poland and end of Polish independence.
1796-1797	Bonaparte invades Italy. Defeat of Austrians.
1797	Reorganization in Italy. Treaty of Campo-Formio.
1798	Establishment of Roman and Helvetic Republics.
1798	Bonaparte's expedition to Egypt. Battle of the Nile (French fleet destroyed by Nelson).
1799-1801	Second Coalition against France.
1799	French defeats on Rhine, in Switzerland, and in Italy.
1799	Coup d'état of 18th Brumaire (Nov. 9). Directory overthrown. Constitution of Year VIII. Bonaparte First Consul.
1799-1804	Consulate in France. Bonaparte practically dictator.
1800	Bonaparte's second Italian campaign (Marengo).
1801	Peace of Lunéville. French frontier extended to Rhine.
1801	Concordat (Pius VII and France).
1802	Peace of Amiens (Great Britain and France).
1803	Renewal of war between Great Britain and France.
1804	Publication of Code Napoleon.
1804	Napoleon proclaimed Emperor of the French.
1805	Third Coalition against France (Great Britain, Russia, Austria, Sweden).
1805	Surrender of Austrian army at Ulm.
1805	Battle of Trafalgar. Nelson destroys French sea-power.
1805	Battle of Austerlitz. Austria and Russia defeated by Napoleon.
1805	Peace of Pressburg. Napoleon master of Italy.
1806	Confederation of the Rhine set up by Napoleon. Formal end of the Holy Roman Empire.
1806	War declared by Prussia against Napoleon. Battles of Jena and Auerstadt. Humiliation of Prussia.
1806	Berlin Decrees. Beginning of Continental System.
1807	Battle of Friedland. Collapse of resistance to Napoleon by Prussia and Russia.
1807	Peace of Tilsit.
1808-1814	Peninsular War (Spain and Great Britain against Napoleon).
1809	Austrians defeated at Wagram. Peace of Vienna (or Schönbrunn).
1810	Annexation of Holland to France.
1812	Napoleon's invasion of Russia and disastrous retreat from Moscow.
1813	Battle of Leipzig. Napoleon defeated. Allies begin invasion of France.
1814	Capture of Paris by Allies. Napoleon abdicates.
1814	Restoration of Bourbons (Louis XVIII).
1814	Congress of Vienna opens (September).
1815	Return of Napoleon from Elba.
1815	The Hundred Days. Napoleon defeated at Waterloo; exiled to St. Helena.
1815	General reorganization of Europe by Congress of Vienna.

1815-1849

1815	Quadruple Alliance to enforce treaty. Holy Alliance (Alexander I of Russia).
1817	Underground liberal movement in Germany. Wartburg **Festival**.

1818	Congress of Aix-la-Chapelle. Withdrawal of army of occupation from France.
1819	Carlsbad Decrees suppressing liberalism. Reaction in England. "Six Acts."
1820	Liberal uprising in Spain.
1820	Congress of Troppau.
1820	Cato Street Conspiracy in England.
1821	Congress of Laibach.
1821	Liberal uprising in Italy crushed.
1821-1829	Greek War of Independence.
1822	Congress of Verona.
1823	French intervention in Spain to crush liberal revolt.
1823	Monroe Doctrine.
1827	Turkish fleet destroyed by English, French, and Russians at Navarino Bay.
1828-1829	Russo-Turkish War.
1829	Treaty of Adrianople. Greek independence.
1830	July Revolution at Paris. Louis Philippe, King of the French. Charles X deposed.
1830-1832	Revolt in Poland suppressed.
1830-1833	Belgian revolt against Dutch successful.
1832	Reform Bill in England.
1834	German customs union (*Zollverein*).
1838-1848	Chartist agitation in England.
1839-1842	Opium War (Great Britain, China).
1840	Penny post established in England.
1840-1848	Ministry of Guizot in France. Growing discontent.
1845-1846	Famine in Ireland.
1846	Repeal of Corn Laws in England.
1848	*Communist Manifesto* (Karl Marx, Friedrich Engels).
1848	February Revolution in Paris. Second French Republic. Revolutionary movements in Milan, Vienna, Berlin.
1848	Metternich resigns.
1848-1849	Austro-Sardinian War (Charles Albert).

1849-1914

1851	Coup d'état of Louis Napoleon.
1854-1856	Crimean War (Great Britain, France, Turkey against Russia).
1856	Treaty of Paris.
1857	Sepoy Rebellion in India.
1858	Plombières Agreement (Cavour, Napoleon III).
1859	War of France and Sardinia against Austria. Battles of Magenta and Solferino. Withdrawal of Napoleon III (Truce of Villafranca).
1859	*Origin of Species* (Charles Darwin).
1860	Tuscany, Parma, and Modena join Sardinia.
1860	Expedition of Garibaldi to Sicily.
1861	Victor Emmanuel II king of Italy. All Italian peninsula except Venice and Rome united.
1861	Emancipation of serfs in Russia.
1861-1867	French intervention in Mexico.
1861-1890	Prince Bismarck leader in Prussia and German Empire.
1864	Austro-German seizure of Schleswig-Holstein.
1866	Seven Weeks' War (Prussia, Austria). Battle of Sadowa (Königgratz). Italy annexes Venetia.

1867	Second Reform Bill in England (urban workingmen enfranchised).
1867	Federal union of Dominion of Canada.
1867	Ausgleich (Austria-Hungary).
1867	First volume *Das Kapital* (Karl Marx).
1870	Doctrine of Papal Infallibility.
1870-1871	Franco-German War. Battle of Sedan. Abdication of Napoleon III. Third French Republic.
1870-1871	Annexation of Rome to Kingdom of Italy.
1871	United German Empire.
1871	Treaty of Frankfurt.
1871	Uprising of Paris Commune crushed.
1872	Ballot Act in England.
1873	May Laws against Catholics in Germany.
1873-1875	Civil disorder in Spain.
1875	Great Britain acquires control of Suez Canal.
1875	Constitutional Laws of Third French Republic.
1876	Revolts in Balkans against Turks. Bulgarian massacres.
1877-1878	Russo-Turkish War.
1878	Congress of Berlin. Settlement of Eastern affairs. Austrian administration of Bosnia-Herzegovina.
1879-1887	Jules Grévy, President of French Republic. End of serious monarchist effort.
1881	Alexander II of Russia assassinated (Nihilists, Terrorists).
1883	Triple Alliance formed (Germany, Austria, Italy).
1886	First Home Rule Bill defeated (Gladstone).
1887-1889	Boulangist agitation in France.
1890	Resignation of Bismarck.
1891	Anti-Semitic pogroms (Russia).
1891	Encyclical *Rerum Novarum* (Leo XIII).
1891-1902	Trans-Siberian Railway.
1892	Dual Alliance (France, Russia). Strengthened 1894.
1894-1899	Dreyfus Case.
1894-1896	Armenian massacres.
1895	Jameson Raid (South Africa).
1896-1899	Cretan revolt. Turco-Greek War.
1898	Large scale naval program in Germany.
1898	Fashoda Incident (France, Great Britain).
1898	Spanish-American War.
1899	First Hague Conference.
1899-1902	South African (Boer) War.
1904-1905	Russo-Japanese War.
1904	Rupture between French government and Vatican.
1904	Anglo-French Entente Cordiale.
1905	Revolution in Russia. Duma conceded.
1905	First Moroccan Crisis.
1905	Separation of Sweden and Norway.
1906	Conference of Algeciras (Moroccan question).
1907	Anglo-Russian agreement. Foundation of Triple Entente.
1907	Second Hague Conference.
1907	Encyclical *Pascendi* condemning modernism.
1908	Annexation of Bosnia-Herzegovina by Austria.
1911	Parliament Act in Great Britain.
1911	Agadir Incident.
1911-1912	Turco-Italian War.
1912	Failure of Haldane Mission (Naval reduction).
1912	Anglo-French Entente strengthened.
1913	Balkan Wars. Military preparedness fever.

1914-1963

1914	Outbreak of World War. Battle of the Marne.
1915	Russian defeats in East. Failure of Dardenelles campaign. Deadlock in West.
1916	Struggle for Verdun. Somme offensive by British.
1916	Rumania enters war.
1917	United States enters war.
1918	Treaty of Brest-Litovsk. Final German effort in West.
1918	Armistice signed.
1919	German Republic.
1919	Peace of Paris. League of Nations.
1921-1922	Washington Conference. 5:5:3 naval ratio agreed upon.
1922	Fascist coup places Mussolini in power in Italy.
1923	French occupation of Ruhr. German financial collapse.
1923	Corfu Incident.
1924	Dawes Reparations Plan.
1924	Death of Lenin precipitates struggle for power in Soviet Union.
1925	Locarno Treaties.
1926	Admission of Germany to League of Nations.
1928	Five Year Plan begun in Soviet Union.
1929	Lateran Treaty solves "Roman Question."
1929	Young Plan for settlement of reparations.
1929	Collapse of stock prices, beginning of world depression.
1930	Evacuation of Rhineland.
1931	Republic in Spain.
1932	Conference of Lausanne.
1933	Nazi dictatorship in Germany (Adolf Hitler).
1934	"Blood Purge" in Germany.
1934	Attempted Nazi coup in Austria. Assassination of Premier Dollfuss.
1935-1936	Italo-Ethiopian War. Sanctions voted by League of Nations.
1936	Remilitarization of Rhineland.
1936	Outbreak of Spanish Civil War (Francisco Franco).
1937	Japan begins conquest of China.
1938	Germany annexes Austria.
1938	Czechoslovakian Crisis. Conference of Munich.
1939	German Russian Mutual Assistance Pact.
1939	Britain and France declared war on Germany.
1939-1940	Russo-Finnish War.
1940	German conquest of Denmark, Norway. Luxembourg, Holland, and Belgium.
1940	Fall of France.
1941	German invasion of Russia. Japanese raid on Pearl Harbor.
1941	United States declared war on Japan, Germany, and Italy.
1945	Surrender of Germany.
1945	First atomic bomb used. Surrender of Japan.
1946	United Nations convenes. UN Disarmament Resolution.
1948	Communists seized control of Czechoslovakia.
1949	North Atlantic Pact.
1950	Korean Crisis.
1955	German sovereignty.
1956-1957	Suez Canal crisis.
1958	European Common Market.
1961	Russia's Gagarin first man in space.
1961	Berlin Wall.
1962	Algerian independence.
1963	France vetoes Britain's application for membership in the Common Market.

Chief European Rulers
Since 1500

Albania
1478-1913,	Part of Turkey
1913-1914,	William of Wied, prince
1918-1)27,	Republic
1928-1939,	Zog I
1939-1943,	Part of Italy
1943-1945,	Provisional Government
1945- ,	Republic

Premier:
1945-1954,	Enver Hoxha
1954- ,	Mehmet Shehu

Austria
1493-1519,	Maximilian I
1519-1520,	Charles I (V as Holy Roman Emperor)
1520-1564,	Ferdinand I
1564-1576,	Maximilian II
1576-1612,	Rudolph V (II as Holy Roman Emperor)
1612-1619,	Matthias
1619-1637,	Ferdinand II
1637-1657,	Ferdinand III
1658-1705,	Leopold I
1705-1711,	Joseph I
1711-1740,	Charles II (VI as Holy Roman Emperor, III of Hungary)
1740-1780,	Maria Theresa
1780-1790,	Joseph II
1790-1792,	Leopold II
1792-1835,	Francis I (II as Holy Roman Emperor)
1835-1848,	Ferdinand I (IV of Hungary)
1848-1916,	Francis Joseph
1916-1918,	Charles I (IV of Hungary)
1918-1938,	**Republic**
1938-1945,	Annexed to Germany
1945- ,	Republic

President:
1945-1950,	Dr. Karl Renner
1951-1957,	Theodore Koernor
1957- ,	Adolf Schaerf

Belgium
1516-1713,	Part of Spanish Monarchy
1713-1797,	Part of Austrian Monarchy
1797-1815,	Part of France
1815-1830,	Part of Netherlands (Holland)
1831-1865,	Leopold I
1865-1909,	Leopold II
1909-1934,	Albert
1934-1944,	Leopold III
1944-1950,	Prince Charles (Regent)
1951- ,	Baudouin I

Bulgaria
1393-1878,	Part of Turkey
1879-1886,	Alexander, prince
1887-1908,	Ferdinand I, prince
1908-1918,	Ferdinand I, king
1918-1943,	Boris III
1943-1946,	Regency
1946- ,	Republic

Courland
See Latvia

Croatia
1102-1918,	Part of Hungary
1918- ,	Part of Yugoslavia

Czechoslovakia
1471-1516,	Ladislaus II
1516-1526,	Louis
1526-1918,	Part of Austria - Hungary
1918-1939,	Republic
1939-1945,	Annexed to Germany
1945- ,	Republic

Presidents:
1920-1936,	Thomas Masaryk
1936-1948,	Dr. Emil Benes
1948-1952,	Klement Gottwald
1952-1957,	Antonin Zapotocky
1957- ,	Antonin Novotny

Denmark
1481-1513,	John
1513-1523,	Christian II
1523-1533,	Frederick I
1533-1559,	Christian III
1559-1588,	Frederick II
1588-1648,	Christian IV

1648-1670,	Frederick III
1670-1699,	Christian V
1699-1730,	Frederick IV
1730-1746,	Christian VI
1746-1766,	Frederick V
1766-1808,	Christian VII
1808-1839,	Frederick VI
1839-1848,	Christian VIII
1848-1863,	Frederick VII
1863-1906,	Christian IX
1906-1912,	Frederick VIII
1912-1947,	Christian X
1947- ,	Frederick IX

Estonia

1346-1561,	Part of Estates of Teutonic Knights
1561-1721,	Part of Swedish Monarchy
1721-1917,	Part of Russian Empire
1918-1940,	Republic
1940- ,	Constituent Republic of U.S.S.R.

Finland

1290-1809,	Part of Swedish Monarchy
1809-1917,	Part of Russian Empire
1919- ,	Republic

France

1461-1483,	Louis XI
1483-1498,	Charles VIII
1498-1515,	Louis XII
1515-1547,	Francis I
1547-1559,	Henry II
1559-1560,	Francis II
1560-1574,	Charles IX
1574-1589,	Henry III
1589-1610,	Henry IV
1610-1643,	Louis XIII
1643-1715,	Louis XIV
1715-1774,	Louis XV
1774-1792,	Louis XVI
1792-1804,	First Republic
1804-1814,	Napoleon I, emperor
1814-1824,	Louis XVIII
1824-1830,	Charles X
1830-1848,	Louis Philippe
1848-1852,	Second Republic
1852-1870,	Napoleon III, emperor
1870-1940,	Third Republic
1940-1945.	Vichy Government
1945-1958,	Fourth Republic
1958- ,	Fifth Republic

Presidents:

1871-1873,	Adolph Thiers
1873-1879,	Marshall MacMahon
1879-1887,	Jules Grévy
1887-1894,	F. Sadi Carnot
1894-1895,	Casimir-Périer
1895-1899,	Félix Faure
1899-1906,	Émile Loubet
1906-1913,	Armand Fallières
1913-1920,	Raymond Poincaré
1920-1921,	Paul Deschanel
1921-1924,	Alexandre Millerand
1924-1931,	Gaston Doumergue
1931-1932,	Paul Doumer
1932-1940,	Albert Lebrun

Vichy Dictators:

1940-1942,	Marshal Pétain (Chief of State)
1942-1945,	Pierre Laval (Dictator)

Presidents:

1945	Charles de Gaulle
1946	Felix Gouin
1946-1947,	George Bidault
1947-1954,	Vincent Auriol
1954-1958,	René Coty
1958- ,	Charles de Gaulle

Germany

Up to 1806,	Part of Holy Roman Empire
1815-1866,	Part of Germanic Confederation
1871-1888,	William I
1888	Frederick III
1888-1918,	William II
1918-1934,	Weimar Republic
1934-1945,	Nazi Dictatorship
1945-1955,	Allied Occupation

Presidents, Weimar Republic:

1919-1925,	Friedrich Ebert
1925-1934,	Paul von Hindenburg

Fuehrer:

1934-1945,	Adolf Hitler

Federal Republic of Germany
President:

1949-1959,	Theodore Heuss
1959- ,	Heinrich Luebke

Chancellor:

1949- ,	Konrad Adenauer

German Democratic Republic
President:

1949-1960,	Wilhelm Pieck

Chancellor:

1949- ,	Otto Grotewohl (Minister-President in 1960)

Great Britain

Sovereigns of England, 1485-1707

1485-1509,	Henry VII
1509-1547,	Henry VIII
1547-1553,	Edward VI
1553-1558,	Mary I
1558-1603,	Elizabeth I
1603-1625,	James I (VI of Scotland)
1625-1649,	Charles I
1649-1660,	Republic (Oliver Cromwell)
1660-1685,	Charles II
1685-1688,	James II (VII of Scotland)
1689-1694,	William III and Mary II
1694-1702,	William III
1702-1714,	Anne (Queen of Great Britain after 1707)

Sovereigns of Great Britain, 1707-1801

1707-1714,	Anne
1714-1727,	George I
1727-1760,	George II
1760-1820,	George III, (King of Great Britain and Ireland after 1800)

Sovereigns of Scotland, 1488-1707

1488-1513,	James IV
1513-1542,	James V
1542-1567,	Mary
1567-1625,	James VI (I of England, 1603-1625)
1603-1707,	Successions as in England

Sovereigns of the United Kingdom of Great Britain and Ireland 1801—

1801-1820,	George III
1820-1830,	George IV
1830-1837,	William IV
1837-1901,	Victoria
1901-1910,	Edward VII
1910-1936,	George V
1936 ,	Edward VIII (abdicated)
1936-1952,	George VI
1952- ,	Elizabeth II

Prime Ministers of Great Britain since 1868:

1868-1874,	William E. Gladstone
1874-1880,	Benjamin Disraeli
1880-1885,	William E. Gladstone
1885-1886,	Marquess of Salisbury
1886	William E. Gladstone
1886-1892,	Marquess of Salisbury
1892-1894,	William E. Gladstone
1894-1895,	Earl of Roseberry
1895-1902,	Marquess of Salisbury
1902-1905,	Arthur J. Balfour
1906-1908,	Sir Henry Campbell-Bannerman
1908-1916,	Herbert H. Asquith
1916-1922,	David Lloyd George
1922-1923,	Andrew Bonar Law
1923	Stanley Baldwin
1924	J. Ramsey MacDonald
1924-1929,	Stanley Baldwin
1929-1935,	J. Ramsey MacDonald
1935-1937,	Stanley Baldwin
1937-1940,	Neville Chamberlain
1940-1945,	Winston Churchill
1945-1951,	Clement Attlee
1951-1955,	Winston Churchill
1955-1957,	Anthony Eden
1957- ,	Harold Macmillan

Greece

1453-1829,	Part of Turkey
1829-1832,	Republic
1832-1862,	Otto I
1863-1913,	George I
1913-1917,	Constantine I
1917-1920,	Alexander I
1920-1922,	Constantine I (restored)
1922-1924,	George II
1924-1935,	Republic
1935-1941,	George II (restored)
1941-1944,	German Occupation
1944-1946,	Archbishop Samaskino (Regent)
1946-1947,	George II (restored for second time)
1947- ,	Paul

Holland

See Netherlands

Holy Roman Empire

1493-1519,	Maximilian I
1519-1558,	Charles V
1558-1564,	Ferdinand I
1564-1576,	Maximilian II
1576-1612,	Rudolph II
1612-1619,	Matthias
1619-1637,	Ferdinand II
1637-1657,	Ferdinand III
1658-1705,	Leopold I
1705-1711,	Joseph I

1711-1740,	Charles VI
1742-1745,	Charles VII
1745-1765,	Francis I
1765-1790,	Joseph II
1790-1792,	Leopold II
1792-1806,	Francis II (after 1804 Francis I, Emperor of Austria)

Hungary

1490-1516,	Ladislaus II
1516-1526,	Louis II
1526-1918,	Part of Austrian Monarchy
1918-1920,	Republic
1920-1946,	Kingdom
1946- ,	Republic

Regent:

1920-1944,	Admiral Horthy

Presidents:

1946-1948,	Zoldan Tildy
1948-1952,	Arpad Szakasits
1952- ,	Istvan Dobi

Ireland

1922-1937,	Self-governing Dominion of British Empire
1937- ,	Republic

Presidents:

1938-1945,	Douglas Hyde
1945-1959,	Sean T. O'Kelly
1959- ,	Eamon de Valera

Italy

Kings of Sardinia

1720-1730,	Victor Amadeus II
1730-1773,	Charles Emmanuel III
1773-1796,	Victor Amadeus III
1796-1802,	Charles Emmanuel IV
1802-1821,	Victor Emmanuel I
1821-1831,	Charles Felix
1831-1849,	Charles Albert
1849-1878,	Victor Emmanuel II
1861- ,	As King of Italy

Kings of Italy

1861-1878,	Victor Emmanuel II
1878-1900,	Humbert
1900-1946,	Victor Emmanuel III
1946- ,	Republic

Dictator:

1922-1943,	Benito Mussolini

Presidents.

1946-1948,	Enrico de Nicola
1948-1955,	Luigi Einaudi
1955-1962,	Giovanni Gronchi
1962- ,	Antonio Segni

Latvia

1237-1549,	Part of Estates of Teutonic Knights
1549-1629,	Part of Polish Monarchy
1629-1721,	Part of Swedish Monarchy
1721-1917,	Part of Russian Empire
1918-1940,	Republic
1940- ,	Constituent Republic of U.S.S.R.

Lettland

See Latvia

Lithuania

1501-1793,	Independent Part of Polish Monarchy
1793-1917,	Part of Russian Empire
1918-1940,	Republic
1940- ,	Constituent Republic of U. S. S. R.

Livonia

See Latvia

Montenegro

1696-1735,	Danilo, prince-bishop
1735-1782,	Sava and Vasilije
1782-1830,	Peter I
1830-1851,	Peter II
1851-1860,	Danilo I, prince
1860-1910,	Nicholas I, prince
1910-1918,	Nicholas I, king
1918- ,	Part of Yugoslavia

Netherlands

1516-1581,	Part of Spanish Monarchy
1581-1584,	William the Silent, stadholder
1584-1625,	Maurice
1625-1647,	Frederick Henry
1647-1650,	William II
1650-1672,	John De Witt, grand pensionary
1672-1702,	William III, stadholder (King of England and Scotland 1689-1702)
1711-1747,	William IV, nominal stadholder
1747-1751,	William IV, hereditary stadholder
1751-1795,	William V
1795-1806,	Republic
1806-1810,	Louis Bonaparte, king

1810-1813,	Part of France
1813-1840,	William I, king
1840-1849,	William II
1849-1890,	William III
1890-1948,	Wilhelmina
1948- ,	Juliana

Norway

1397-1814,	Part of Danish Monarchy
1814-1905,	Part of Swedish Monarchy
1905-1957,	Haakon VIII
1957-	Olav V

Poland

1492-1501,	John I Albert
1501-1506,	Alexander I
1506-1548,	Sigismund I
1548-1572,	Sigismund II
1573-1574,	Henry of Valois (Henry III of France)
1575-1586,	Stephen Báthory
1587-1632,	Sigismund III Vasa
1632-1648,	Ladislaus IV
1648-1668,	John II Casimir
1669-1673,	Michael Wisniowiecki
1674-1696,	John III Sobieski
1697-1704,	Augustus II
1704-1709,	Stanislaus Leszczynski
1709-1733,	Augustus II
1733-1734,	Stanislaus Leszczynski
1734-1763,	Augustus III
1764-1795,	Stanislaus II Poniatowski
1795-1918,	Partitioned among Russia, Prussia, and Austria
1918-1939,	Republic
1939-1945,	Partitioned by Germany and Russia
1945-1946,	Provisional Government
1947- ,	Republic

Popes, The

1492-1503,	Alexander VI
1503	Pius III
1503-1513,	Julius II
1513-1521,	Leo X
1522-1523,	Adrian VI
1523-1534,	Clement VII
1534-1549,	Paul III
1550-1555,	Julius III
1555	Marcellus II
1555-1559,	Paul IV
1559-1565,	Pius IV
1566-1572,	Pius V
1572-1585,	**Gregory XIII**

1585-1590,	Sixtus V
1590	Urban VII
1590-1591,	Gregory XIV
1591	Innocent IX
1592-1605,	Clement VIII
1605 ,	Leo XI
1605-1621,	Paul V
1621-1623,	Gregory XV
1623-1644,	Urban VIII
1644-1655,	Innocent X
1655-1667,	Alexander VII
1667-1669,	Clement IX
1670-1676,	Clement X
1676-1689,	Innocent XI
1689-1691,	Alexander VIII
1691-1700,	Innocent XII
1700-1721,	Clement XI
1721-1724,	Innocent XIII
1724-1730,	Benedict XIII
1730-1740,	Clement XII
1740-1758,	Benedict XIV
1758-1769,	Clement XIII
1769-1774,	Clement XIV
1775-1799,	Pius VI
1800-1823,	Pius VII
1823-1829,	Leo XII
1829-1830,	Pius VIII
1831-1846,	Gregory XVI
1846-1878,	Pius IX
1878-1903,	Leo XIII
1903-1914,	Pius X
1914-1922,	Benedict XV
1939-1958,	Pius XII
1958-	John XXIII

Portugal

1495-1521,	Emmanuel (Manoel) I
1521-1557,	John III
1557-1578,	Sebastian
1578-1580,	Henry
1580-1640,	Part of Spanish Monarchy
1640-1656,	John IV
1656-1667,	Alfonso VI
1667-1706,	Pedro II
1706-1750,	John V
1750-1777,	Joseph
1777-1786,	Maria I and Pedro III
1786-1816,	Maria I
1816-1826,	John VI
1826	Pedro IV
1826-1828,	Maria II
1828-1834,	Miguel

1834-1853, Maria II
1853-1861, Pedro V
1861-1889, Louis I
1889-1908, Charles I
1908-1910, Manoel II
1910-   , Republic

ussia
Electors of Brandenburg
1499-1535, Joachim I
1535-1571, Joachim II
1571-1598, John George
1598-1608, Joachim Frederick
1608-1619, John Sigismund
1619-1640, George William
1640-1688, Frederick William
1688-1701, Frederick III (as Frederick I, King of Prussia, 1701-1713)

Kings of Prussia
1701-1713, Frederick I
1713-1740, Frederick William I
1740-1786, Frederick II
1786-1797, Frederick William II
1797-1840, Frederick William III
1840-1861, Frederick William IV
1861-1888, William I (German Emperor, 1871-1888)
After 1871 part of German Empire

umania
1500-1856, Part of Turkey
1861-1866, Alexander John Cuza, prince
1866-1881, Charles I, prince
1881-1914, Charles I, king
1914-1927, Ferdinand I
1927-1930, **Michael**
1930-1940, **Carol**
1940-1947, Michael (abdicated)
1948-   , Republic

ussia
1462-1505, Ivan III
1505-1533, Basil IV
1533-1584, Ivan IV
1584-1598, Theodore
1598-1605, Boris Godunov
1613-1645, Michael Romanov
1645-1676, Alexius
1676-1682, Theodore II
1682-1689, Ivan V and Peter I
1689-1725, Peter I

1725-1727, Catherine I
1727-1730, Peter II
1730-1740, Anna
1740-1741, Ivan VI
1741-1762, Elizabeth
1762   , Peter III
1762-1796, Catherine II
1796-1801, Paul
1801-1825, Alexander I
1825-1855, Nicholas I
1855-1881, Alexander II
1881-1894, Alexander III
1894-1917, Nicholas II
1917-1923, Republic
1923-   , Union of Soviet Socialist Republics

Dictators: (Communist):
1917-1924, Nicholas Lenin
1924-1953, Joseph V. Stalin
1953-1955, Georgi Malenkov
1955-1958, Nikolai A. Bulganin
1958-   , Nikita S. Krushchev

Scotland
See Great Britain

Serbia
1459-1830, Part of Turkey
1804-1813, Karageorge, prince
1817-1839, Milosh
1839   , **Milan**
1839-1842, Michael
1842-1858, Alexander
1858-1860, Milosh
1860-1868, Michael
1868-1882, Milan, prince
1882-1889, Milan, king
1889-1903, Alexander
1903-1921, Peter
1918-   , Part of Yugoslavia

Slavonia
See Croatia

Slovakia
See Czechoslovakia

Sloveniva (Carniola, etc.)
1300-1809, Part of Austrian Monarchy
1809-1813, Part of French Empire
1813-1918, Part of Austrian Monarchy
1918-   , Part of Yugoslavia

Spain
1479-1504, Ferdinand and Isabella
1504-1506, Ferdinand and Philip I

1506-1516,	Ferdinand and Charles I
1516-1556,	Charles I (V of Holy Roman Empire)
1556-1598,	Philip II
1598-1621,	Philip III
1621-1665,	Philip IV
1665-1700,	Charles II
1700-1746,	Philip V
1746-1759,	Ferdinand VI
1759-1788,	Charles III
1788-1808,	Charles IV
1808-1813,	Joseph Bonaparte
1813-1833,	Ferdinand VII
1833-1868,	Isabella II
1870-1873,	Amadeo of Savoy
1873-1875,	Republic
1875-1885,	Alphonso XII
1886-1931,	Alphonso XIII
1931-1939,	Republic

Presidents:
| 1931-1936, | Niceto Zamora |
| 1936-1939, | Manuel Azâna |

Dictators:
| 1939- , | Francisco Franco |

Sweden
1397-1523,	Part of Danish Monarchy
1523-1560,	Gustavus I Vasa
1560-1568,	Eric XIV
1568-1592,	John III
1592-1604,	Sigismund
1604-1611,	Charles IX
1611-1632,	Gustavus II Adolphus
1632-1654,	Christina
1654-1660,	Charles X
1660-1697,	Charles XI
1697-1718,	Charles XII
1718-1720,	Ulrica Eleonora
1720-1751,	Frederick I
1751-1771,	Adolphus Frederick
1771-1792,	Gustavus III
1792-1809,	Gustavus IV
1809-1818,	Charles XIII
1818-1844,	Charles XIV
1844-1859,	Oscar I
1859-1872,	Charles XV
1872-1907,	Oscar II
1907-1950,	Gustavus V
1950- ,	Gustavus VI

Turkey
1451-1481,	Mohammed II
1481-1512,	Bayezid II
1512-1520,	Selim I
1520-1566,	Suleiman II
1566-1574,	Selim II
1574-1595,	Murad III
1595-1603,	Mohammed III
1603-1617,	Ahmed I
1617-1618,	Mustapha I
1618-1623,	Othman II
1623-1640,	Murad IV
1640-1648,	Ibrahim
1648-1687,	Mohammed IV
1687-1691,	Suleiman III
1691-1695,	Ahmed II
1695-1703,	Mustapha II
1703-1730,	Ahmed III
1730-1754,	Mahmud I
1754-1757,	Othman III
1757-1773,	Mustapha III
1773-1789,	Abdul Hamid I
1789-1807,	Selim III
1807-1808,	Mustapha IV
1808-1839,	Mahmud II
1839-1861,	Abdul Medjid
1861-1876,	Abdul Aziz
1876	Murad V
1876-1909,	Abdul Hamid II
1909-1918,	Mohammed V
1918-1922,	Mohammed VI
1923- ,	Republic

Presidents:
1923-1938,	Kemal Ataturk
1938-1950,	General Ismet Inonu
1950-1960,	Celal Bayar
1960- ,	Cemal Gursel

Union of Soviet Socialist Repub
See Russia

Yugoslavia
1918-1921,	Peter I (King of Serbia 1903-1918)
1921-1934,	Alexander I
1934-1946,	Peter II (Regency Council)
1946- ,	Federated Republic

Dictator
| 1946- , | Marshall Tito (Josip Broz) |

BIBLIOGRAPHY

Artz, F. B., *Reaction and Revolution, 1815-1832*. rev. ed. New York: Harper and Brothers, 1934.

Becker, Carl, *The Heavenly City of the Eighteenth Century Philosophers*. New Haven: Yale University Press, 1932.

Berkeley, G. F. H., *Italy in the Making*. 3 vols. Cambridge: Cambridge University Press, 1932-1943.

Brinton, Crane, *A Decade of Revolution, 1789-1799*. New York: Harper and Brothers, 1934.

————, *Ideas and Men*. New York: Prentice-Hall, 1950.

Bruun, G., *Europe and the French Imperium, 1799-1814*. New York: Harper and Brothers, 1938.

Bruun, G. and H. S. Commager, *Europe and America Since 1492*. Boston: Houghton Mifflin, 1954.

Cassirer, Ernst, *Philosophy of the Enlightenment*. Boston: Beacon Press, 1955.

Clark, G. N., *The Seventeenth Century*. 2nd ed. New York: Oxford University Press, 1947.

Clough, S. B., *Basic Values of Western Civilization*. New York: Columbia University Press, 1960.

Clough, S. B., *Economic Development of Western Civilization*. New York: McGraw Hill, 1959.

Contemporary Civilization Staff of Columbia College, *Introduction to Contemporary Civilization in the West*. 2 vols. New York: Columbia University Press, 1946.

Curtis, E., *History of Ireland*. 6th ed. New York: Barnes & Noble, 1950.

de Tocqueville, Alexis, *The Old Regime and the French Revolution*. Stuart Gilbert, tr. New York: Anchor Books (Doubleday and Co., Inc.), 1955.

Dietz, F. C., *The Industrial Revolution*. New York: Henry Holt and Co., 1927.

Dorn, W. L., *Competition for Empire, 1740-1763*. New York: Harper and Brothers, 1940.

Ergang, R., *Europe Since Waterloo*. 2nd ed. Boston: D. C. Heath and Co., 1961.

Fuller, J. F. C., *A Military History of the Western World*. Vol. II. New York: Funk & Wagnalls, 1955.

Gershoy, Leo, *From Despotism to Revolution, 1763-1789*. New York: Harper and Brothers, 1944.

Grant, A. J., *A History of Europe, 1494-1610*. 5th ed. New York: Barnes & Noble, Inc., 1951.

Grimm, H. J., *The Reformation Era*. New York: Macmillan Co., 1954.

Guerard, Albert Leon, *France, A Short History*. New York: W. W. Norton & Co., 1946.

Halecki, Oscar, *A History of Poland*. rev. ed. New York: Roy Publishers, 1955.

Hammond, J. L. and B., *The Rise of Modern Industry*. London: Methuen Co., 1947.

Harbison, E. Harris, *The Age of the Reformation*. Ithaca: Cornell University Press, 1955.

Hazard, P., *European Thought in the Eighteenth Century*. New Haven: Yale University Press, 1954.

Hoffding, Harald, *A History of Modern Philosophy*. B. E. Meyer, tr. 2 vols. New York: Dover Publications, 1955.

Kirchner, Walther, *History of Russia*. 3rd ed. New York: Barnes & Noble, Inc., 1963.

Kirchner, Walther, *Western Civilization Since 1500*. New York: Barnes & Noble, Inc., 1958.

Kohn, Hans, *Making of the Modern French Mind*. Princeton: Anvil Books (D. Van Nostrand Co.), 1955.

———, *Nationalism, Its Meaning and History*. Princeton: Anvil Books (D. Van Nostrand Co.), 1955.

Legge, J. C., *Rhyme and Revolution in Germany, 1813-1850*. London: Constable & Co., Ltd., 1918.

Lucas, H. S., *The Renaissance and Reformation*. 2nd ed. New York: Harper and Brothers, 1960.

Marriott, J. A. R., *The Eastern Question*. 4th ed. Oxford: Oxford University Press, 1940.

———, *Evolution of Modern Europe, 1453-1939*. London: Methuen Co., 1944.

———, *A Short History of France*. New York: Oxford University Press, 1944.

Marriott, J. A. R. and C. G. R. Robertson, *Evolution of Prussia*. rev. ed. New York: Oxford University Press, 1946.

Ogg, D., *Europe in the Seventeenth Century*. 8th ed. New York: Macmillan Co., 1960.

Ogg, F. A. and W. R. Sharp, *Economic Development of Modern Europe*. New York: Macmillan Co., 1950.

Pares, Sir Bernard, *Russia*. 6th ed. New York: New American Library, 1955.

Reddaway, W. F., *History of Europe, 1610-1715*. New York: Barnes & Noble, Inc., 1948.

Roberts, P., *The Quest for Security, 1715-1740*. New York: Harper and Brothers, 1947.

Salvemini, G., *The French Revolution, 1788-1792*. New York: W. W. Norton & Co., 1962.

Smith, Preserved, *Age of the Reformation*. New York: Henry Holt & Co., 1920.

Steinberg, S. H., *History of Germany*. Cambridge Press, 1944.

Sypher, Wylie, *Four Stages of Renaissance Style, 1400-1700*. New York: Anchor Books (Doubleday and Co., Inc.), 1955.

Taylor, A. J. P., *The Course of German History*. New York: Coward-McCann, Inc., 1946.

———, *The Habsburg Monarchy*. 2nd ed. New York: Macmillan Co., 1949.

Taylor, F. S., *From Napoleon to Stalin*. London: Hamish Hamilton, Ltd., 1950.

———, *A Short History of Science and Scientific Thought*. New York: W. W. Norton and Co., 1949.

Trawick, Buckner B., *World Literature*. Vol. II. New York: Barnes & Noble, Inc., 1955.

Trevelyan, G. M., *History of England*. 3rd ed. New York: Longmans, Green and Co., 1945.

Wallbank, T. W. and A. M. Taylor, *Civilization Past and Present*. Vol. II. 4th ed. Chicago: Scott Foresman Co., 1960.

Webb, S. and B., *History of Trade Unionism*. rev. ed. New York: Longmans, Green and Co., 1920.

Willey, Basil, *The Seventeenth Century Background*. New York: Anchor Books (Doubleday and Co., Inc.), 1953.

Index